BISON
BOOKS

AMERICAN LIVES | *Series editor*: Tobias Wolff

LIZ STEPHENS

# The Days
# Are Gods

. . . . . . . . . . . . . . . .

University of Nebraska Press | Lincoln & London

Portions of "So Manifest It, Man" and "The Magic Trick"
first appeared as "Ten Years I'll Never Get Back," *Fourth
Genre* 12, no. 2 (Fall 2010): 27–37. © 2010 by Liz Stephens.

"Utah Looked Like This to Me" first appeared in
*South Dakota Review* 43, no. 3 (Fall 2005): 27–38.
© 2005 by Liz Stephens.

Manufactured in the United States of America

Publication of this volume was assisted by a grant from
the Friends of the University of Nebraska Press.

Library of Congress Cataloging-in-Publication Data
Stephens, Liz, 1968–
The days are gods / Liz Stephens.
p. cm. — (American lives)
ISBN 978-0-8032-4354-5 (pbk.: alk. paper) 1. Stephens, Liz,
1968– 2. Community life — Utah — Wellsville. 3. Wellsville
(Utah) — Social life and customs. 4. Wellsville (Utah) —
Biography. 5. West (U.S.) — Social life and customs. I. Title.
F834.W45S74 2013
979.2'12 — dc23        2012035999

Set in Minion by Laura Wellington.

No one expects the days to be gods.

RALPH WALDO EMERSON

# CONTENTS

...............

# PROLOGUE

.................

Our real estate agent, Brady, tells me he'll have a kid go by to water our lawn until we move up, since there is a month between when we bought the house in Utah and when we'll be moving in. I'm standing in the kitchen of our Los Angeles house listening to passing traffic, traditional Mexican polka music on car radios waa-waaing closer to us and then waa-waaing away, and I'm picturing a patchy lawn we've bought in the Rocky Mountains, where there is no traffic, no fence, no edge, which just peters out into a gravel road crossed by cows. "He's real dependable," Brady tells me. How much, I ask. "Free," he says.

I tell Christopher when I hang up the phone. "He says a kid will water the lawn. For free."

"Huh," Chris says.

The day we drive in, a snarling mess of dog hair and snack wrappers, four men stand in our front lawn. In Los Angeles before we left I'd spent a day haggling with movers on the phone long distance, unable to figure out why no major moving companies worked in Cache Valley, Utah, abutting Idaho and Wyoming. "They're here to help," Brady says on moving day. "Just friendly."

Christopher and I have no prepared facial expression for this. We must look as we feel: blank. "I called the bishop of the local ward, and he put the date of your move into the church bulletin, and these gentlemen came to help," Brady says. I have barely enough energy reserved for the translation this requires into my own language, where Episcopalian bishops preside over whole sections of states and one never meets them and one is never sure what they do. And wards are in hospitals. And the word *church* often makes people walk away. And "help," from strangers? Forget about it, there was nearly no translation.

By the time these men are talking among themselves about how to get someone over with a pulley to raise our mattress into the tiny upstairs bedroom, as it will not fit up the narrow hundred-year-old staircase, talking about this as if it were fun, Christopher and I are just doing whatever they tell us to. It is not the last time we will feel like ineffectual children here. By the time they leave, the truck is only holding hot L.A. air, and we have been offered breakfast next door at our neighbor's house. When that neighbor had come by to offer breakfast, we'd said conversationally, "Nice cat," of the tabby winding around her ankles. "Ah, no," she said, looking pointedly at the hole cut into the back door of our garage. "That's your cat."

"Is this weird?" I ask Christopher.

The men had looked out of the corner of their eyes at us, no doubt about it. What do they see? Here's me: All direct eye contact and rambling sentences, conversation that veers toward the overly familiar. Secondhand boys' clothes. (Stuff they can't see: tattoos, a constant battle against hermeticism that borders on misanthropic, a mean interrupting streak.) Here's Christopher: Visible tattoos. Jeans trod right out at the heel. Stained T-shirt perfect for moving day. Aggressive niceness. (What they can't see: juvenile delinquency, innumerable bar fights, member of AA.) We know the open-handed generosity of these people must not be as simple as it seems. It must come with the kind of judgments people always give other people, once they are at home at their own kitchen tables. But while they are standing there with us, it's welcoming, and calming. And it got our truck unloaded. A new Utah Mormon friend will in fact remind us in the near future that even Mormons can be mean behind your back, but Chris only snorts. "Being nice to our face is great." He won't be there to listen, he points out, the rest of the time.

Brady gave us a key to the house as he left.

We will never use the key once.

That evening standing in our own backyard, gaga at all the stars we haven't seen since childhood, I jump out of my skin when a horse across the road floats up to the fence in the blackness, scratching her side against the wire. "Holy mother of God," I snap, throwing my hands in front of myself in the dark. The ease and size and silence of her moving in the near-pitch dark reminds me of sharks in mile-deep water, bogeymen in children's books. And then there is the spit of a sole ATV crunching gravel as it passes, and then nothing. Our heartbeats.

# 1

## LOS ANGELES

...................

# HOT AIR

................

kept wondering when that tiny Mexican dog would show up. Perhaps it was too hot, even for him. One hundred and ten degrees, out in prime Southern California wildfire country under a crud-brown smoggy sky, was certainly the kind of weather the news anchors told you to stay out of unless absolutely necessary. But here we were, a crew of about eighty grown-ups all too dumb to quit a job that forced us to carry heavy equipment in the heat under the direction of yelling despots, for the ultimate higher purpose of selling Taco Bell food to apathetic gringos.

The set was on Melody Ranch, which I'd been told was built for Gene Autry's horse in the 1940s. Though I wanted this to be true, that Autry had built an actual Old West town for the horse to wander through, a sort of Marie Antoinette of animals, the only part of the story that turned out to be right was the connection to Autry. He had purchased the place after filming his movie *Tumbling Tumbleweeds* there in 1935, and then rented it out for filming to other companies. *Gunsmoke* was filmed there, along with many of John Wayne's movies, dozens of other lesser-known projects, and (after I'd been there) *Deadwood*. And now here we sat, the production crew for a Taco Bell commercial, and at the end of the experience we'd have a T-shirt to show for it that read "This town ain't big enough for the all of us: Taco Bell." A little magenta-and-orange bell logo sits haphazardly next to a brown bucking bronco on the back of the shirt.

My jobs on television commercial sets changed regularly, and I did craft service on this shoot, which means I was in charge of snacks. This job is just as grand as it sounds: lots of good perks (dog food and laundry detergent on Taco Bell's tab when I went shopping) but decidedly "below the line." In ten years, I never knew just what people in Los Angeles meant by this phrase — I think it may be a reference to the way names are displayed on movie posters — but I knew I was below it for sure. On the other hand, because most people who work "in the industry" are fairly sure that people who don't talk loud enough can't hear either, and so many people in Hollywood don't eat anyway, I often loved my nearly invisible position, tucked behind a chip- and chocolate-laden table, which was behind, in this case, the false front of a circa 1850s post office.

Though I couldn't find the sombrero-clad Chihuahua on the set (I pictured him in a director's chair near a fan somewhere in the shade), I was drawn each day to the Western extras. Always separate from everyone else, surrounded by gear that is all their own and they supply for a price — huge sheepskin chaps, extra saddles, stiff reining ropes hanging coiled on trees and trailers — they glided at a remove from our sweaty, petty work-a-day reality. Add to this the fact that these men (almost always men) were tending to their horses at all times, exotic and threatening animals to nearly everyone else on the set. High girlish shrieks and giggles were heard regularly from this side of the "town" whenever anyone else, with their cell phones clamped to one ear, wandered unwittingly too near the back end of these dusty generic brown animals, their other hand thrown up in defense against a calmly grazing horse.

And this, it seemed to me, as a newcomer from Chicago, was the West.

It took a day to set up the main stunt. Men are fighting in the saloon, in predirtied reproduction clothes, over a card game. One man pushes another during a fight, with enough force to send him flying out of the front plate-glass window, where he lands in the hard pack of the street. Somehow this has something to do with tacos.

What most people who watch commercials or movies don't think about is that chances are if you are — if the camera is — in front of a building, that building has no insides. From Capra's *It's a Wonderful Life* to *High Noon*, these warmly lit homes and well-lived-in towns are empty shells, each shell filled with scaffolding on which to hang lights meant to fill the space with a warm and inhabited glow. Grips and electricians crouch on the catwalks drinking Mountain Dew, waiting for their cues.

Not so this saloon. Over the past fifty years, art departments assigned to previous film and commercial projects had hung Mason jar chandeliers, meticulously faux-aged the mirrors, left smoky oil lamps on hardy old wooden tables. Surrounded by these props, our Western extras were set in place, with the stunt men and fight choreographers whispering from a low out-of-sight spot. If you squinted your eyes, it was pretty great. Not perfect, but effective.

Of course, I was barely allowed into the saloon, below the line as I was (only allowed in to bring the actors bottles of water between takes), and I was generally consigned to sneaking up behind the director and the clients (the Taco Bell advertising people) where they sat in their tent, attended by production assistants who moved fans ever nearer their above-the-line faces. As I stood holding trays of fruit smoothies, or tiny quiches, I could crane my neck around the script supervisor's shoulder to watch the action, not as it actually happened in front of me ten yards away, but on the monitor. Here we all focused, twenty of us or so, leaning intently in to watch the flickering video screen, twelve or fourteen inches of perfect Old Western reproduction.

The Western extras were apparently worth every dime. So authentically grizzled, so slouchy and yet quick-draw-alert in their body language, they instantly brought to mind an entire body of work, often because they had themselves appeared in whatever Western in which you might imagine them. Sure, of course they brought to mind the real Old West too, where a man's saddle might be the most expensive single thing he ever owned, and he might never marry, due to lack of funds and, well, women. In addition, those historical cowboys were mostly transient (a word that in Los Angeles now means "homeless schizophrenic people that roam downtown"). But these modern Hollywood cowboys almost certainly lived in one place, and most likely it was one of three: Shadow Hills, Chatsworth, or Burbank itself, the only places within easy working distance of Los Angeles with horse property. Though in Burbank now you couldn't have your horse with you, naturally — this would be roughly equivalent in Angelenos minds' with having a jet plane, or a merry-go-round, the stuff of fantasies. No, horses are kept at the Burbank Equestrian Center; the smell of horse manure wafting in the air made one particular intersection near the freeway seem downright rural. I had cause to remember this often after moving away, then transient myself, in part because of the stark contrast between my later actual rural life and the former weekends I'd spent roaming horsey parts of the city, but not least because I myself owed (still owe) the Burbank Equestrian Center seventy dollars.

The hard-packed dirt in front of the saloon had been covered unobtrusively with what production art departments the world over know as Fuller's Earth, a dun-colored man-made mineral powder so light it catches the air at the slightest provocation. This creates magical billowing clouds of dust — in this case, creating the effect that the man thrown from the window has hit the ground seriously hard, hard enough to scatter the horses tied out front. But the horses were in fact pulled out of frame by trainers, since show horses are inevitably trained to stand still for anything, even their natural flight instinct duplicated on cue when required.

Similarly, no one was throwing an expensive, insured, and union-protected featured extra (that's the person himself, carefully not called an actor because then he has to be paid more) out any window. In one shot, the camera captures the well-worn hands of a man grabbing the coat of another, a close-up of dirty fingernails curling around the rough "home-spun" cloth. There is a jerk, one shake of a fight. In the next shot, the camera has moved much closer to the director's tent to reveal a medium-wide angle of the plate-glass window. Not too many takes can be done of such a setup, since the time-intensive replacing of plate glass in a large window frame is prohibitive. So for one take, I watch as stunt men pull, with measured force, the Western stunt extra (double pay for this one, with double specialties, Western and stunt — yes, "Western" distilled down to a payable skill) from inside the window by a rope, giving his body just the right jerk of surprise, just the right extra velocity of a real body throw. He leaps into the air to assist the movement, throwing himself with the trained grace of a ballet dancer into a jackknife, out of a glass window backward, into the deceptively soft-looking puff of Fuller's Earth on earth.

The second take I watch through the monitor, over the director's shoulder. This is the true entertainment on a boring set, to jockey into viewing position, to watch a shot on the set, and then to see "how it works" on the monitor.

It works perfectly. I have no idea what it has to do with tacos, but it looks completely real, as Old West bar fights go. Or rather went. Supposedly, according to movies I have seen. I have been given a rare glimpse of history with dust, grunting, clanking spurs, and the smell of sweat, a sort of virtual reality blip of history. I marvel at how well we do what we do; how given hundreds of thousands of dollars, the manpower of about a hundred people, three or four weeks of preproduction, and a day in the desert in a well-constructed ghost town, and snacks, Hollywood can make thirty seconds of (revisionist, reductive) history happen again.

Some days, I remember as if it's a dream the days I worked on sets. Sometimes I even worked on sets within sets — Paramount, Warner Brothers, Universal. On the Universal lot, a trolley takes tourists on a trek through the sound stages, away from the themed rides and candy. I'm sure for a visitor it feels so, well, real, to be back away from the hubbub, watching extras in nurse costumes, zombie outfits, flapper dresses, spilling from the elephant doors of the stages out into the sunlight for lunch. Sometimes these tourists would point at me, sweaty and exhausted, hovering at the flashing red "cameras rolling" light outside a sound stage door as their trolley breezed by, and I'd find myself suddenly self-conscious, studiously attentive to performing my mundane job, as being viewed can make one do, for people who saw it as magical, one of the cogs of the movie system. Not an important cog, of course, or else why would I be carrying a twenty-pound bag of dripping ice and a tray of lattes?

. . .

Long hills of late-season hay roll away from me. I squint at this largess from under my shady canopy. I am surrounded by tables of food. Sun-hot food that I've been shooing flies off of for hours. Nobody should want this food. And yet, here I sit, just in case somebody can't find the protein bars or the chips. What a ridiculous business television commercial making is. Everyone is so serious on the job, you'd think it was brain surgery.

But we shoot in beautiful locations. This is a ranch in Malibu, the kind of place my cattle-raising relatives in Oklahoma might dream about. I've worked here on shoots intended to sell music, razors, medication, television shows. We have all been here, with a variety of film crews, over and over again. Apparently, this view sells a lot. The ranch manager comes by on his horse while I sit glaring at the traveling circus I came in with: camera vans, props trucks, "honey wagons" (semi-trucks full of toilets), tables and chairs, plus couches and fans and espresso machines. I know I got there with the mess, but I judge us. "It's lovely here," I tell him, about everything up there on the ranch besides us. "Oh, yes," he agrees. "And you should be here in the early evening, when the coyotes are howling while the wind picks up."

"Wow," I say. "There are coyotes out here?" I am encircled by miles of open range, light shade cover, the occasional clear stream, hundreds and thousands of field mice, and small perfect foods for coyotes. *Miles* of open land.

He looks at me like I'm a child. And maybe not a smart one. "Uh, yeah."

I am standing in a dim bar in Shadow Hills, California, and the owner is sitting on a bar stool looking away from me. This would be unremarkable except for one thing: I have just asked him a question. The half dozen locals who sit with him at the bar go silent. He stares pointedly away. I look at the bartender. "Really?" I say out loud, to her, to him, to all of them. It's the best I can muster.

Back at our table, I look at the three friends with whom I rode motorcycles out to this place. My boyfriend, Christopher, and I have been looking into renting a house out here, one of the last bastions of country within regular driving distance of Los Angeles. We drive through the area nearly every weekend gazing in something like disbelief at the trailers and log homes perched like an after-thought next to dusty paddocks and horse barns. We want in.

But apparently, even though rental agents and real estate agents are happy to talk, this guy isn't having it. I've asked him for directions and it's perfectly fitting, actually, that he won't give them to me. Ripe for metaphor, he literally won't tell me how to get around this place where he lives, how to get deeper in. He's just going to ignore that the question is out there.

Sadly, it won't matter that he, one individual, won't help me, one individual. The city slickers are coming anyway. This is not the kind of place that Angelenos, hungry for something novel, won't find, too inexpensive to ignore, too scenic to leave alone.

I wish he could see me for what I *feel* I am, someone who values what he's trying to protect, someone who just wants to live quietly on her own little dusty horsy corner. Not build a huge show house, or try to change zoning when I realize belatedly I don't like the smell of manure, or whatever his fears are. But the fact is, we're both right. I can come out here if I want to, with or without his blessing. And he can dislike me for it, just on sight, on principle.

Nevertheless. It's a little disheartening to know I've got city, don't-know-what-I'm talking-about, and unwelcome written all over me. He'll never know the irony of how hard I worked to get that city shine, relatively small-town girl that I was, and how happy I'd be now to give it up, how tired I am of carrying it. I try to simultaneously see myself from outside and inside my skin, from my hurry-up and pay-your-way-in paradigm to an alternate don't-hurry-but-don't-rest and pay-your-dues mind.

The road I was looking for, by the way, was the one on which the bar sat.

The blast of cold air that hits us as we enter this place that calls itself "the last honky-tonk in the San Fernando Valley," distracts us for a second from noticing we have walked into the middle of the dance floor during a two-step lesson. The instructor, balding, heavy-set, but only thirty, pauses the music on the boom box set on the edge of the stage, which leaves the bar silent except for the shuffle of shoes. "Hiya," he says, his finger hovering over the pause button. We are surrounded by old people, and they are all looking at us. The women wear frilly skirts that look as if they were made for dolls. The gentlemen hitch their slacks under their belt buckles, and the swinging begins again. We are obviously in the way, so we move back to the free buffet of meatballs and chicken wings.

Again, sensory overload, this time of dealing with lukewarm food on a bendy paper plate while trying to look as if we do this every happy hour, distracts us momentarily from looking out the propped-open back door where a few hardened gals smoke on the cement parking lot, milling about the handicap spot. Distantly, across the dimming evening tarmac, we hear and then see a mule, tied to a hitching post.

It's hard work, being country in Los Angeles.

But we're committed. We start to drive out there a lot; we

become familiar with the aloof rich Mexican woman of a certain age who wears boots that cost what most of us make in a week, familiar with the strangely optimistic dance instructor, and the man who comes alone to dance quickly and indiscriminately with young ladies. We can almost get out of the way, after a while, as we all two-step madly around the wooden floor. The night the mule's rider brings him in the back door for a drink by the buffet, we are there.

Other friends begin to wonder why in the world we drive out to the valley so often. They are playing pool in West Hollywood, but we are square dancing with people older than their parents.

But nobody out there ever asks us what we do, or how successfully we're doing it. They don't care who we know, or tell us who they know. Mostly, they grab our hands and make us dance, or refill our Mason jars with more iced tea and whiskey. There's a lot of nodding hello — not waving, nodding; I am reminded of a line from a memoir I've just read on ranch life: "I never saw a man raise his arms above his shoulders unless it was to ward off a blow."

As such, when other younger whippersnappers like ourselves show up, other couples in just the right snap-front shirts and down-at-the-heel boots, driving up on a kitsch-and-irony-hunt from Hollywood, we eye each other accordingly. I might pat the mule possessively, scratch its neck like I know what it likes. "We belong here," I realize I want to tell them. "Look at me talking to this old fogey. Look at me drinking my whiskey out of my Mason jar. Look at my man: yes, that's him, hanging out with the good old boys plugging chew on the back stoop."

Originally, I'd moved to Los Angeles for the same reason everyone does. I wanted excitement. I also wanted to officially join the club of the other people who'd been too weird for high school, but not weird enough to drop out. All the personalities who were too awkward to be convenient or too eccentric or loud or bossy for anywhere else, the people in each of their families who'd seen too many movies and believed too many magazines, often at the high price of paying more attention to actual events. I'd always felt a little odd in the Midwest. It didn't seem to want me any more than I wanted it. But I fit right in, in California.

Still, years after that initial relief, immersed and immured in the isolated Nag Champa-incense-scented ocean-lulled island that is Los Angeles, I was out of touch. I'd stayed in the sun too long. There was a lot of life outside in the big wide world, which I was missing sitting in Thai restaurants, chatting at dog parks, and navigating dense traffic, caught up completely in Hollywood's mythology of itself as the center of the universe.

Los Angeles was a town where I'd heard waiters talk about their movie deals with Paramount, carpet shampooers brag about their auditions with Scorsese. Let me not mislead you — I loved it the whole time. I do love that California welcomes all comers, the odd and eccentric, the dreamers, from high schools, local colleges, and video-store jobs all over America. Nevertheless I felt like I was cheating. Living in a place where I could get away with anything. Pretend there were no seasons, and thus no time passing.

But now I wanted to be somewhere where what people did was what they did. I was tired of glib. I was tired of ironic. I was tired of feeling like life was going to start just as soon as I got an agent (when, in fact, I wasn't even searching for one, but I always felt like I should be). After all, we each only have so much time, and I don't mean that in the sense that trends and the personalities that attend them live and die, or we are only hireable before a certain age, both very Los Angeles notions. I mean it in the big sense: humans die. We only have so much time.

I had lived ten whole years in California as if these were one year, on a loop. But I gradually began to disdain my most steady job, its patent unreality or disconnection with anything that mattered and the way it made me feel like Hollywood's version of the salty gal waitress who would age with admirable resignation, doling wisdom to others without making huge and wonderful decisions about herself: "Sit down, kid, you need a green tea, is what you need." Dilettante visits to the vaguely ruralish parts of the valley were just not going to cut it anymore. I ran my hands over my first gray hairs. I watched toddlers at parks with capable moms who looked like they knew a thing or two. I watched friends of mine take over whole companies, or drop out of acting to follow other more personal dreams, or become celebrities, or dog walkers, or cancer survivors. But the most vivid sign of time passing in my life was the aging of my dogs. Ten years of being twenty-four was enough. I wanted out.

# SO MANIFEST IT, MAN

.................

I was impressed by the way the horses ignored us. Whole film crews might stand shoulder to shoulder in a barn out in the San Fernando Valley; Sharon Stone, or John Cleese, or Matthew McConaughey might lean in a studiously casual manner on the door of a horse's stall while a camera rolled, and still the horses only looked away. (Conversely, there is the production manager of the shoot on which we filmed Matthew McConaughey, as he walked in: "I think," she whispered, sotto voce, "that I just came back out of menopause.")

Not to mention, the way the barns and farmhouses and old mission buildings we often shot in were better than us: more useful, longer lasting, evocative of something mindful, something more meaningful than Gillette razors, than shampoo, Honda, whatever we were there to film ads for. I'd walk out of the hot, hot rooms where the fraught and frantic film crew stood, crouched, ran in circles, and shouted, and an echoing silence sprang up from stone floors; a dense history of other people always stood by until the film crew left again.

What I was seeing, as I worked on these commercial and movie film crews, while I was new to California, was the history of the place around me. While other people were checking lists of props for scenes, watching the camera operators for slight signs of dissatisfaction, juggling sheaves of filming permits under the eye of local sheriffs, I was wandering off from the back, prying open feed bins and closet doors and garden gates. I was hiding in fields of tall grass like I'd never seen, hunched outside my truck on "an errand" down a nearby dirt road, gazing in shock at the acres of sage surrounding me. I never looked into live people's stuff, I should be clear. I'd had enough of live people right behind me hovering over a camera, no doubt looking for me and calling, "Latte!" It wasn't for the people that I felt the deep love. Generally speaking, that is; I adored my friends, other misfits who seldom judged, and when they did judge did so loudly where you could argue with it and call them to toe the line or defend its breach. We had a sort of vagabond honor that had little to do with manners and more to do with ethics. But in short, I was still negotiating with proper people. I was shockingly inept at that, having been allowed to languish in my youth's extended summer vacation. What I was looking for, I finally concluded, was embedded in *the stuff*. Part of the landscape. Maybe if when I'd moved there I'd been faced with Spanish missionaries and vaqueros and schoolmarms, John Wesley Powell pushing his hat back off his forehead with his good arm, everything would have turned out differently.

I applied for graduate school in northern Utah.

I wanted to be a writer, and not of television scripts or publicity promos, jobs other friends did but that again required engaging with a whole industry about which I felt ambivalence. Maybe somewhere deep within my hobby of paying attention — to ranchers I met on shoots, to old farmhouses with views of state highways, to the only other way of life I'd seen people feel heartfelt about besides the Hollywood you-can-check-out-but-you-can-never-leave lament of California — maybe *there* was something to care about. Maybe that weight of attention would yield my own heartfelt heart, to me.

Though Christopher knew I'd applied to grad school, of course, that application felt theoretical, yet another Hollywood pot shot at hope; when I told him months later I'd been accepted, he bristled visibly, horrified at being faced with an actual choice. He stalked out of the house in a huff, walked around the block, and then came back in and said, "Okay." I don't know what I'd have done if he'd said no; I didn't think about it. We'd been gliding along in that seasonless place, where no one will ever press you to make a choice of any kind, where if they did you could just walk away from their bad mojo into the sunshine and the nodding agreement of dozens of other people who refused to be pushed. It was the easiest thing you can imagine to not choose direction, and in that vein, not get married.

We'd been together six years without feeling any particular hurry, but finally we wanted to get married with the friends we knew around us, so we had to get it done right then. And getting married and then immediately moving together was exciting. I wouldn't *recommend* it to anyone; I cried a lot, lost all our bills, messed up a billion details of the way I'd wanted the wedding to be, nearly forgot to pack my computer and then nearly forgot to unpack it before the truck drove away, was extremely sharp with my new in-laws at the wedding when I discovered them feeding my dogs table scraps. I was not at my best.

But once you move away from all you know, the person you are left standing there with is your team. As in us against them. As in knowing where to pass the ball when the other one can make the stronger play. As in go team.

The wedding had, though I blush to say it, a country theme. I am not — swear to God, I am not — a dried-flowers, checked-wallpaper-borders type of girl. I do not particularly like the color dusty blue and am not a collector of baskets. Nevertheless, shined but used horse shoes were the party favor. To these was attached, with rough twine, stamped in brown ink on tan paper, this saying: "The harder I work, the luckier I get." Seemingly, this had nothing to do with love, but Christopher and I already knew it did. Plus, that saying was going to get us through, we hoped, the next many years of figuring out what the hell we wanted from the rest of our lives. We were done waiting for it, or just occasionally remembering, between naps and sushi, to go at it half-cocked.

The wedding was at our home, where so many friends had spent so much time. There was a bluegrass band, vintage table-cloths with camping lanterns in a big white tent, a perfect cake covered in real flowers that only cost as much as one of my legs, barbecue and cobbler and mint juleps. Christopher wore white Chuck Taylors and a seersucker suit and did not faint. I carried magnolias and wore a dress that felt as good as pajamas. When a slatted metal truck began to circle the place during the ceremony, though I had told not one soul about my surprise, people began to stir. They had zero doubt that a stock truck lost in the streets of Los Angeles was my doing. After photographs, when Christopher and I stepped out the back of our house in the middle of Hollywood, there was a petting zoo on the driveway, just as I'd ordered it, surrounded by hay bales and feed buckets and sixty or so of the most gleeful urban adults you've ever seen. They had been taking photographs since the pig first put her delicate hoof down the unloading deck.

The owners of the animals stood by amazed. Kids never had so much fun. By the time we were pulling motorcycle burnouts in the intersection and waving sparklers in the dark, even our caterer from the nearby barbecue joint had driven slowly by, reporting later to her husband that it "looked like a street fair." Someone took a picture of me riding behind Christopher on his motorcycle, coyly clutching a hen against the front of my white dress.

It turned out Christopher thought I'd bought him all the tiny visiting animals. Not yet, I told him.

My first entrance into that valley in northern Utah, when we drive up to look for a house, I experience in a trance of disbelief, in cinematic scale in my mind: Seeing the mountains rise far away from our car on the narrow highway and then sweep close to draw us in with a nearly audible suck — *thup* — into the mouth of Sardine Canyon above Brigham City. The sudden span of fields in the middle of the pass, one metal building crouched in the fold of a distant foothill implying only a human attempt at dominion but not conveying success. My mounting excitement on actually coming into the valley above Logan, looking down on a town of which I could see each edge, where barns and cultivated fields surrounded the bulk of the town and spread out like a flat and shiny puzzle, giving way unevenly to untended land. With the glow of unintended imperialism, I know when I see the sign for a historic tabernacle in Wellsville that I am headed for the right place, the kind of place I knew existed from the movies: Real Rural Historic Places.

Events that are normal for this place seem contrived for our visit. As we drive up the canyon for the first time, cows are milling across the narrow road, wandering along the river.

"Is that a *cow*? Are these *cows*?" I yell. Christopher cackles hysterically, dodging moving cattle around canyon bends. I crane my neck to look for fence up the mountainside, incredulous that any field might be near enough to this canyon road for a downed fence to matter, but somewhere in this public canyon must be access to a private ranch. The conflation of geography and property rights and real live cow on the highway in front of me boggles. I don't understand. I can't see fence. Is this canyon the edge of open range? *Is* there open range? I roll down my window as we drive by and shoo a cow off the road with my hand, giddy.

As we gain elevation on this late May day snow begins to fall in heavy handfuls. We haven't seen snow in years, in Los Angeles. (To put this in perspective, the last time I'd visited my folks in the winter in the Midwest, there'd been no snow but I had stopped in my tracks at the sight of an icy puddle. "Ice," I said loudly.) So now we are giddier than ever, pulling over the car as we approach the top of the mountain pass in order to stand in the wind and hold out our bare hands into the air. Bear Lake is blue below us, the only blue I've ever seen that could almost make me use the word *cerulean*. The snow falls on us but through the snow we see the sun shining on the valleys below.

We stop on the way down the canyon back into town and Christopher puts his fly rod line into the shining river. In five minutes he catches trout. The picture I take is a man fully flummoxed at his own happiness. We both quickly hold the fish before he lets it slip away. "That must be," I say, watching the fly rod cast back into the waters, still feeling the wiggle, "the closest you get to just plugging your hands into the whole world."

At the end of the canyon before we exit, having circled back, two trucks are parked in the rocks and two ranchers, surrounded by milling cows, are craning their necks to see up the side of the mountain.

I learn from the brochures on my bedside table at our hotel

those first nights that Cache Valley was so named because trappers, the first white men in the valley, cached their pelts here, returning to sell these at a yearly mountain man rendezvous. I learn as well that this rendezvous is reenacted annually, and I know I will have to attend "these kinds" of events. I am intent on gathering experiences and am picturing the photos I'll take at each. I am not above imagining how these photos will look to my friends back in Los Angeles. I hope for occasions, and thus photographs, with horses. Some of these pictures might even feature snow, deeply exotic to the folks back in L.A. And snow, of course, might require special outfits, sure to photograph well, as evidenced by the endless photos always available of movie stars decked in obscenely furry boots and long expensive faux-rugged coats (completely unmanageable if doing anything besides standing still; if, for instance, walking through snow) at the Sundance Film Festival in Park City, Utah.

I notice as well, away from government-issue explanatory place markers and nearly impossible to photograph as strikingly as they appear in person, resisting my impulse to document them, the silver glint of the rivers and marshes and irrigation ditches spiderwebbing the valley floor. Even a newcomer can see it was this water that allowed any settling in the valley itself, surrounded as it is by desert outside the protective embrace of the mountains. The combination of strategically man-made and natural paths for this water is irrelevant to me at first, but I am immediately drawn by its influence and to the surprise of it, the shine it has to a person from desert-dry Southern California. Rivers feel brand new: the way the water carries the privacy and mystery of the top of those mountains down to the valley floor, the organic smell, the rush of water moving and then the fecund fertility of it still.

In truth, I guess I was drawn also to water's unmanageability, the fact that charm and showmanship could not be heaped upon the plainly practical and yet ephemeral surface, and the lost and hidden nature of its path. That locals must know the course of these rivers, the sink of these marshy spots, from their fishing and making-out childhoods and teenage years, appealed to me, surprised as I always was by the presence of the water around any corner. Locals even controlled it, with head gates and "water masters" and "water turns" and blue tarps weighted with rocks and twisted into irrigation ditches as dams, directing water toward something only the landowners themselves, and maybe scientists, fully understood.

They did not hire someone who understood it, as we might have done in Los Angeles or, for that matter, in my college life previous to that move, which I arrived and departed from expert in nothing. No, many people here knew how to work their water and land because they'd often been learning how since their great-grandfather threw the first rocks in disgust off the field into the hedgerow.

Such a lifelong understanding of one's home landscape, and the abiding love or at least patience that knowledge indicates, was laudable to me, knowing that in my past, we almost all were transplants, all skimming the surface of the land in Los Angeles, pretending it is not a desert, not even part of the natural world, always stunned to find coyotes in our backyards eating our cats.

# 2

## UTAH

. . . . . . . . . . . . . . . .

I want to make it clear that my move did not take me "back to the land" in the conventional sense. I did not strike out on my own to make a go of it with "an acre and a cow." . . . My move was one that took me deep into the meaning of inheritance.

KATHLEEN NORRIS, *DAKOTA: A SPIRITUAL GEOGRAPHY*

# UTAH LOOKED LIKE THIS

................

U tah looked like this to me, when I drove in: First sage breaking out of the desert, and then slowly, rocks. And then pine trees breaking out of the rocks, and miles later, rocks becoming mountains. Mountains embraced by the sky at the top, where the clouds reached down and threw themselves greedily around the peaks. Sheep grazing where it seemed there must be nothing to be had — only sage, again, in the high mountain desert, and a prehistoric-looking tall plant that began green and ended towering in the blackest brown imaginable, in a lethal-looking tassel. Sheep, and then cattle, that would have appeared lonely and lost on so wide a horizon except that each was utterly grounded, felt elemental, and, if possible, unconcerned. Similarly, from inside the car I began to feel wind-swept, thin-skinned, with a clear-eyed calm emerging from the traffic-snarled many-highwayed past behind me.

When we drove through the town in which we knew we would live, I saw yards I read as haphazard (later I would know better) containing a dog pen, a goat pen, and a trampoline set flush against the back door. The driveways of farmyards in huge gravel arcs dropped back from the road to the privacy of the side door and then back to the business of getting out on the road. I craned my neck for every farmhouse (I would lay my head, my neck, gently onto my hotel room pillow later, demanding not to be asked to look at anything on the television), sure that some key to the whole place would be there in the dirt between barn and house yard, the negative space I couldn't decipher, couldn't get my head around wasting. A dachshund running to meet her boys from off the school bus nearly put me in tears, I was looking so hard for home. I owned dachshunds too; later I would know how impractical they were out in ranch country, bellies dragging in the snow, feet hurt easily, always nearly being trampled by horses, rolled by horns of goats, hating barn cats, useless at keeping up when hiking, barking skittery hot-house flowers of dogs I kept inside (and loved on with ferocity, knowing I can't get the breed again now till I'm ancient and not going anywhere outside, barking mad and skittery myself).

And this image stood out: a boy running down his crescent of a driveway, into a holler where a house waits. I see him hightail it down from one angle — we drive past a crowd of cottonwoods — and craning my neck back I see him met at the door by a little sister and, best, half a dozen sheep, milling on the porch. Sister's hand resting idly on a warm wooly back as it coasts by. This may mean nothing to you, local as you are, to wherever you're from. Everything in me reached out for that. Cottonwoods, curved road, boy, girl, sheep, dog, home, running.

It must have been about three o'clock, if the boy was just getting home. The light was gold like that. It lit up the inside of my brain, my mind's eye, I guess, for days.

Maybe where I've been is coloring my new impressions: I look up the foothills from my new mountain home for a movie set cemetery, set at a discrete and healthy distance, ready with plots for the victims of Main Street shoot-outs and sick babies. And the first time I see a gray, worn barn leaning against the wind, clinging to its mountain ground, high enough to be in snow when the valley bottom was green, a blinding image of gray, dark white, green, and darkening sky, I laugh out loud, into the cold wind off the snowmobile on which I'm rushing by. I've seen that movie, the one with the barn in the mountains. I've read that book, the one with the treacherous winter. And now I am really there.

Still, the first time I see a horse pawing the snow, I feel, beyond expectations, some essential thing fall into place. I can examine the existential sense of the beast, pawing stoically at the deep snow, a cyclical harshness, a sense of the way horses have moved across the plains for ages, pawing through snow for any grass they can get, a tribal memory. But maybe it's just something I've seen in the movies? No, it is more. It is life or death, actually. It is real.

But it's not for nothing I've seen *High Noon* a zillion times; I appreciate immediately what I've got here in this landscape: it doesn't have to "grow on me"; it's already fully taken root. I won't be trying to change it like some other transplanted people: the woman who moved in down the road from me, and quickly alerted the city that her neighbor had an illegal buffalo in his pasture — he returned the favor and remedied the problem by shooting the buffalo as it stood in the pasture, just outside the woman's kitchen window.

I want it to stay forlorn out here. I want a keening wind off a mountain unobstructed. I want my horses to have to paw for grass through snow.

I try to untangle my many affections and aims here in my new mountain home, to distill whether it is the idea of the pioneer that my husband and I love (we could do anything new, as long as it's hard), or the idea of the country (we could live anywhere, as long as it's country), or the idea of the West itself (we could live only here, in sight of the mountains, never more than a minute from a fly-fishing stream). Or is it the mythological West we seek?

What are we doing? And what are we doing here?

I do know this. I bought a horse nearly immediately after the move, before I had a trailer to pick it up, before I could even afford a saddle. And when I swing up into the (borrowed) saddle of that horse in my own back pasture, I have a mini-montage of that right leg swing from every Western (and so far, I haven't stopped thinking, "How cool am I, doing this in my own backyard?"). When I lope and remember not to look down at the horse's neck, but look out and around at where I'm going, I know the set of my head exactly, because I've seen it in the movies. When I drag a ten-gallon bucket of water out to the goats' pen, because, yes, I bought goats too, the whole chore is a whole lot more glamorous than it could be, because I see hundreds of nameless women doing the same thing, implicit somewhere in the background of every Zane Grey–Owen Wister–Larry McMurtry novel there is.

Shouldn't I be simply going to school? Isn't being a graduate student keeping me busy enough? The other grad students, the non-Mormon ones anyway, are sitting on the roof patio of the White Owl Tavern drinking low-alcohol beer while I shovel horse crap.

But I am busy. I am looking for a set of stories to inhabit. Shocking and shallow as that may sound, extremely Generation X, adrift on the world and looking for someone else's story to live — well, let's just get it out there. How wrong, or right, is what I'm doing?

My family, like the vast proportion of families today, moved not enough to inhabit a glamorous story of international intrigue, or even the army brat story of incidental dual citizenship, but just enough to water down completely any regional, local identity we might want to claim. My parents come from somewhere, of course; they come from Oklahoma. This is where their childhoods lie, their parents' graves, their own ancestors. But Oklahoma exists for me as a kind of cipher, a repository of memories disconnected from my everyday psyche-forming life, as a place where I place my theoretical family history.

Because they moved, I grew up in the Midwest. I grew up in places where my parents could offer me not many of their family memories, and I was dismissive of my own, unappreciative in the way only kids should be, knowing unconsciously that my childhood was fill-in-the-blank normal in that uncomplicated, entitled way of so many middle-class midwestern white kids. For whatever reason, I spent most of my time biding my time.

But I want a place now. Now that I am grown and know what sort of person I will be, I know what to look for. I don't want to manufacture a jet-set home-is-where-the-heart-is, wherever-I-lay-my-hat comfort. This land, to me, so unlike what I was raised with, is exotic enough. I want to know every weed. And I want to stay where my dogs get buried in the land; I don't want to leave their bones to future willy-nilly garden diggers and house-building improvement makers. I want it to be this land, which reminds me every day to look up.

I should acknowledge, I've seen too many movies. I've read too many books. I've got an overactive imagination. For me, that glamorous cowboy past, that layered and place-specific heavy-with-myths past, is simmering just below the surface of the present. For better or worse, and I know there's some of both. But I want this to work. This new place, I can feel it, is a relationship I want. My internal works, the noisy spinning of my wheels, have already found balm in the overweening arch of this timeless harsh landscape, which births and kills, which demands attention.

So I try to remember I am not in a book. I am not living a movie Western, old or new. I promise I will not be disappointed when ranchers want to move to town or drive ATVs instead of horses to move cattle. I will not be surprised when the local wives look askance at me for talking back to my husband, for being too old to *not* have children. I will not be alarmed that town mayors and town sages sometimes live in trailers, or tract homes. I will not balk at the skinned elk hanging upside down at my neighbor's.

But I already know this interesting thing: I will be disappointed when the rest of the people like me get here, others perhaps more aggressive or less imaginative in their dreams, to make a theme park out of the actual West. I will uproot, and move again, further out, and keep looking.

My new old house, so far, in spite of our mortgage payments, belongs to the neighborhood, the place and the people that have watched the structure's plinths and porch roof lines shift and settle, its lilac bushes grow into monsters. The one hundred years it has sat on this spot make the house more surely part of the earth below it than any piece of paper that says we are in charge.

Folks out strolling past in the evening ask each other in the still, carrying air, "Wonder if they'll paint this place finally?" and, until we got horses onto the pastures, "Hope they use this space. Be a shame not to see it put to use." More than a few people have told us they considered buying our place for the land, and there are some implicit messages in that. One, they had their shot at it and allowed us to have it. Two, they've all seen the inside of our house. Three, the land is worth more than the house. And four, if we don't use the outbuildings and pastures, they may just take it all back. Eminently practical, they'll put animals on the pastures within an hour of our ousting, and the earth itself, and gravity, will take care of the untended barns, and the home.

One neighbor tells us he used to milk cows in the milk house (that's a milk house?) at the back of our property, when he was a boy, with a kid named Tater. My husband's boss's wife grew up in this house; her name is in the concrete of our front stoop. They are unsurprised at this coincidence, one that makes us feel as if the stars have lined up.

When we start work on the inside of the barn, our neighbor Bill only shakes his head and laughs when we discover caches of empty beer cans, a juicy find in Mormon country. He does not tell us the story that his head shaking seems to indicate. We did not buy the rights to the former resident's stories, after all. We just bought the house. Everything else we have to earn.

They look just like normal people, our neighbors. In spite of being Mormon, and rural, well, they look just like normal people. Notice our naiveté is boundless; we have forgotten through years of living in Los Angeles anything we ever might have known about what actually concerns people in their lives outside of cities. We can parallel park like stunt drivers but can hardly hold a conversation about more than a dozen rote topics.

So it took us an hour to get dressed for this picnic, and I still don't think we got it right, trying to look like we didn't have to *try* to be so clean, so not urban, so modest, so church-clothes. No one should sweat as much as we are, trying to enjoy a picnic.

"This is Christopher and Liz," our host says in a gratifyingly kind voice to her other guests. She had knocked on our door yesterday to invite us to this, plunging us headfirst into the locals. They now stared back. Affectionately, it must be said. Still, we sweat.

"What's your last name?" an older man calls out. No one shushes him. Indeed, even the ones closer to our age nod, so I can't attribute this to senility. In Los Angeles, asking this outright is the same as asking how much money you've got; since the first question often answers the second, you ask anyone besides the person themselves what anybody's name is. Besides, unless you really are trying to figure out something mercenary about a person — their profession or show business history — their last name won't matter, because you don't know their family, you just don't. It registers for the first time that we are in a new world where this is polite. I now feel as if we have entered a gauntlet, or a maze.

"Martin," I say. My last name stays dryly in my throat. It has suddenly become "my professional name." I won't explain it.

"Are you related to the . . . ?" someone trails into a full name that doesn't register to me. That's okay, I don't need to hear it to answer.

"No."

It's all right. They keep smiling. But they are not done.

We stand like marionettes in front of a panel of locals, being gently quizzed. Why did we move here? Do we have kids? Do we keep horses? Every single one of our answers is just a little wrong, like when you answer a magazine quiz and you can tell you should choose all the "a" options in order to get the most desirable result but all the "b" options are truer. Martin. For graduate school. No kids. No, we didn't move here with any — horses or children. No, we don't know Kurt Crabtree, from whom we bought the house. Yes, we deduced that they were getting divorced. No, we didn't know he kept draft horses. Yes, we found the deer carcass in the barn.

Over time, all these women will visit my house; I will learn not to sit around in my pajamas, and to always have the dishes done. They will never get used to my dogs being kept inside, rushing them at the door; I will not always eat the food they drop off, the gelatin salads and heavy, sweet, ground beef lasagnas. They will invite me to women's group meetings and gift sales parties and pyramid scheme pitches, until finally sometimes I hide when I see them coming, woman after woman parking in the dirt, walking through my yard to the side door.

Christopher will be asked to disbud (dehorn) calves, weld gates, move hay, walk down loose cows. We will say yes to nearly everything, because when we later need to borrow a trailer, get our paddock harrowed, catch our horses, have gas brought to us when we're stopped on the highway, quietly have our dog buried, these people will be the ones to do it.

On the other hand, we are not given a Book of Mormon for some time, just when Christopher had begun to feel insulted. It was analogous, he said, to going to a gay bar and not being checked out. He wasn't gay, but wasn't it nice to be asked? I think this is funny, but maybe that's just me. Anyway, it's not a story I tell the neighbors, though they are more irreverent, and lusty, and realistic, than I ever thought they would be.

Christopher and I talk right through the beginning of the picnic-food blessing before we eat, because everyone is too polite to shush us, and then suddenly we find ourselves holding hands with strangers, praying by default. We get into the car as evening unravels in the fields between our homes, my lap heaping with leftover cake in a tin with the hostess's name in Magic Marker on the bottom, and garden zucchini I couldn't avoid.

# CHECKING FENCE

..................

Periodically as I explore our new place, I walk to the back of our property. I go back there less often than I thought I would when we bought it, but more often than most of my neighbors visit their own backyards. I'm beginning to realize why real estate agents consider outbuildings a mixed blessing on a listing. On the one hand, they're useful. On the other hand, who uses them? When we'd moved in, I thought we'd have parties under the huge hay shed, string lights along its lowest edge, sit on the hay bales with friends. We haven't yet.

Back under the shed sits Chris's old truck, his Las Vegas coffee mug with a ring of brown dirt at the bottom, bundles of used hog fence and barbed wire, and a couple of stacked tons of hay. The western view from the shed could make a person cry; it's the same view from our kitchen window, but without those surrounding walls, not to mention the dishes and phone calls, the mountains are bigger. The Wellsville Mountains reflect the season of the valley, the degree of snow transmutable to actual information about the goings-on in town. When we moved to Wellsville, there was no snow on the mountain, but we have begun to realize that condition only lasts about two months, August and September. County fair, hunting, snowmobiling, rodeo — you can predict all this according to how far down the side the snow reaches.

From the hay shed (and from the window where my desk sits inside) I can see the town reservoir. I sit on the hay and watch kids fish about a half mile down the gravel road.

To the east of my back field lies the field of my neighbor, divided from us not by a fence but by a wide paddock gate so that the fields can be used to graze animals together or separately, depending on the current state of the relationship between the neighbors. Right now, things are good along those lines, except that the neighbors are trying to make their place look more private than it is, because they want to sell. Technically, they do own their place, so I have not been asked my opinion.

The neighbors to the back of us, right behind the hay shed, never open their shades or curtains. They are known to "have an attitude" and are not listed on the church map of the ward. They always have two hot rods in the crash-up derby.

Across the street from our house is a cow pasture. The house that used to be "attached" to that pasture has been sold separately, and even we can see this is a problem, in that things can happen, as they have here, like the owner of the house doesn't like the cows.

Wandering the back of the property is like archaeology to me. I own, still standing, the last outhouse for my house before inside plumbing came, but for a while the small building seemed to me like an art installation, a sculptural object, meant to make me consider the notion of outhouse in a distant past. But there's the hole inside, no arguing with that, and the bench, though more hog fence and loose boards stand stacked there, presumably to keep them out of the weather for future use, a future that has come and gone both. I measure the distance from the outhouse to my house with my eyes, my feet, my chilly arms, and my wariness of stepping any great distance through the dark. It's a long way from a warm bed to here, even in my imagination.

For a while a harrow belonging to the last owner lay in the weeds back here, until he called us and urgently asked to be let in the fence to take it away. It was his father's he said. Where he put it, when he himself lived in town in a post-divorce apartment, we didn't know. He probably realized he could still sell it.

The barn is more of the same. Other people shoe their horses there. Bill has been inside it more than I have, if you count before I lived here. But I am in there a lot, just not to do the things I imagined I would. Did I think I'd be tacking up horses every day, loping out onto the dirt road beside the paddock? I think so. But not yet. I got chickens instead. I clean the chicken coop, collect eggs, get armloads of flakes of hay to throw in the feeder for the horses we don't ride that are already accruing mysteriously in the paddock, and I stand leaning on the barn gate, staring at sunsets to the west. I've already sat in the barn many days and watched the farrier hammer shoes onto my new horse and others' horses, watch my dog and other people's dogs snatch up the hoof shavings to gnaw them until they give off a nasty, earthy smell. Much in the way I used to sometimes hover just inside the garage while my dad worked on old cars, and then in a shady spot of the driveway while Christopher worked on motorcycles in L.A., happy just to smell and observe and listen, I sit in a corner by my chickens.

The chickens are mine. No one else wants to bother with them, and so no one bosses me about them. They cluster around me when people or dogs are in the barn, pecking my ankles until I swat them. Rushing away and swirling back like water.

# WARY

..................

I know it's silly, the flat-out mark of a city-dweller, but it seems kind of, well, cool, after I've begun to settle in, when I hear pheasants just outside my kitchen window or watch them dodging the horses in the paddock outside my office. My ten-year-old neighbor waves his BB gun at them and looks at me out of a wary sideways eye (the way nearly everyone here looks at us, when they think we aren't looking). I tell him I don't need any favors when he offers to clear the property of magpies. "Even magpies?" he whines, and walks away dragging his gun in what can't be an NRA-recommended fashion. Anyone with sense would know magpies were put on the earth for target practice.

We attend rodeos with the fervor of converts, zealots who now know every rule of calf roping (three legs doesn't count), bronc riding (keep your heels up on her neck), mutton busting (crying's allowed in this event only), and that what the British call scones is not what you get at the state fair rodeo, where scones means Navaho fry bread. We go to a rodeo on the Wyoming state line, the arena set in a bowl of earth partway up a mountain. When we'd got lost looking for it — no signs anywhere, and we didn't know yet that in every town there's a main street, one main cross street, and a riding arena on the edge of town under a couple of big lights you can see at night for miles and miles — we'd rolled down the car window and driven quietly along until we heard an announcer's voice carrying out over the cool late-afternoon air. Not a single person is there *playing* cowboy, wearing the outfit in hopes that someone will see them "being Western" — they just are, hundreds of people standing in this bowl of light that the sunset hits, where at evening, dark spills out the bottom edge to cover the entire plain below. In time, people carry their toddlers like sacks of flour over their shoulders to the car for the long sleepy drive home. I am exquisitely aware that I am not a visitor now. I too am only driving a few miles home, not the thousands of miles in my life it took to get here.

Somewhere in this halcyon time I remember that I am only a local in my own mind. I fret with and try to parse my highly conscious sense of my surroundings, examining it for ironic detachment. But in truth, I am already in over my head: I am already cut loose from the pattern in my life of seeking myself solely in the face of others, so I'm in new territory in every sense. In other words, I thought it would matter more if the locals here liked me, wanted me here, or thought I could hack it. But instead, I expend more effort actually hacking it than thinking about it. I am in love.

It is the landscape that draws me and keeps me here, concurrently spare and breathtaking enough to empty my mind of chatter like hours of meditation I could never sit through. Movies and books were telling me how to read the land before I arrived, but I know I've prepped myself by careful selection of my sources: never mind that thousands of people died or went insane throughout history trying to live the reality of this lyrical idea, the notion that the harshness of the land is pure romantic challenge. You always think you'll be the one to make the living look easy.

Well, not too easy. That wouldn't be any fun.

A new friend of mine wears outlandish clothes, colors her hair in crazy shades, shows so much skin: she's mad at Utah, my newfound home. She's from this culture, and in most ways, she wants out. But she is more likely to be able to fit in here, if only she wanted the free pass. The belonging is built into her. She undoubtedly thinks it's funny that I do want it, and ironic that I think I can get the version that comes without religious conversion. Self-exiled from the tightly embracing community, she resists the dark truth of its patriarchal roots, the homophobia with which the church struggles in its quickly changing present state. Still, she rarely swears, an abstention that is a church rule, and she will not tell me the most secret tenets of Mormonism. "Lightning will hit me," she says and laughs, sort of. She does tell me she used to buy the smallest religious undergarments there were — another church tenet, the garments are a kind of imposed modesty, a constant reminder of one's relationship to the world — and when she felt even that limited her, she started rolling up the cap sleeves and the bloomers' legs. She isn't Mormon anymore.

# AUDELL'S CARPENTER'S AND BUILDER'S GUIDE

.................

**M**andilyn and James live on a beautiful few acres in the middle of the valley, surrounded by tended fields, equidistant between the Wasatch and the Wellsville mountain ranges. I met Mandilyn because her husband owns the tattoo shop in town. I say "because" because having tattoos establishes one as counterculture here in a manner that has worn out in urban centers. She accorded us townie status immediately, kept us from being up on the literal and figurative hill where the university stands, leapfrogged us into the lingo of "wards" and "sister missionary" and "Family Night Mondays," not because she was Mormon but because she had been. Her husband, James, had laconically started a conversation with us on our second visit to town. "I saw you at the rodeo two months ago," he said when we stood paying a bill at the Bluebird diner counter in town. "We did," Mandilyn said. "But I was so pregnant I wasn't feeling chatty."

My husband's first job in the valley has been to weld a six-story tower just off the highway, and it turns out you can see that tower from our friends' yard, the highest eyesore in their view. Those three — Mandilyn, James, and Christopher — see the land around them the way it is now, and why shouldn't they, but with a sixth sense that I hope is only the rattle of paranoia, I see another transparency laid upon our lovely view. As we eat in the shade of their cottonwoods, they hear the chickens and turkeys and goats and pigs and stray cats of their farm, and I can dimly hear the sound of construction and then car horns and people slamming doors. I see fresh concrete driveways. But for now, that's just me.

James is building their house. They live for the present in a trailer, behind which rises slowly the hand-hewn massively formidable skeleton of a home built to last. We sit on the timbers as he saws the notches in, as he hand-drills the peg holes for pegs that he's hand-carved into other thick beams. It is work as slow as it sounds. Mandilyn tells me that she and their young son sit with James outside some days, laying a picnic on the future roof and wall beams of their home; they will all have touched every piece of the place over and over by the time they live in it, some theoretical distant time in the future. They are mostly very patient.

One day James hands me the hand drill he's been using. He nods toward one of the huge beams. "Give it a try," he says.

I sit on the beam, one leg on each side, and set the iron drill onto the wood. "Where did you get this?" I ask.

"eBay," he laughs. "That stuff is going cheap. Nobody wants it."

"It's decorative," Mandilyn chimes in. She makes air quotes with her hands as she says it. They see what our grandfathers would have seen: that tool only needed a little oil.

James resets my drill before I start — "This isn't for fun, I need this hole," he says — and I start turning the hand crank. A foam of fresh wood shavings seems to pour from the top edge of the hole I'm drilling. It smells like I'm sitting on an entire forest, snapping trees in two. Christopher nearly knocks me off the beam in his zeal to do it too. I helped build the house, I think (unrealistically).

"Anytime you want to do more of that, I've got the work for you," James says. We all look at the monstrous pile of beams stacked carefully at the side of the house yard. Covered presently by chickens and turkeys and the scrambling of their toddler son. If you look closely, most beams have already got James's pencil markings, the math of the house traced on the raw material. It all takes so much *time*.

They plant swatches of greenish brown, wisps of flexible sticks, and promise these will rise as trees. In the future, they say, with all the time in the world. Mandilyn shows me *Audell's Carpenter's and Builder's Guide, 1923*, a book as lovingly detailed and loaded with dust and smells of wood as the garage and basement workshops of old men. She is having a plaque made of the frontispiece for the stoop of their future home. It reads: "When we build, we think that we build forever. Let it not be for present delight nor be for present use alone. Let it be such work as our descendants will thank us for: and let us think, as we lay stone on stone, that a time is to come when those stones will be scarred because our hands have touched them, and that men will say, as they look upon the labor and wrought sustenance of them, 'See! This our father did for us.'"

I feel a sort of pain when I read this. I hand the book to my husband, but look away while he reads the page. Mine is an abstract desire, but his is concrete: to build with his capable hands something permanent.

I should mention, to give due credit, that James isn't building the whole house entirely alone. He calls in favors when he absolutely has to. The day Mandilyn drove home from her grandfather's funeral, heart heavy, the driveway and the adjoining road were full of the trucks of people waiting to help raise up the first roof beam.

They are all as enamored of the project as we are — the audacity of a man choosing to build with the twelve-inch square wood beams, raised into place by the hands of men, choosing to build forever in the middle of such valuable real estate, choosing to build forever at all.

# POWWOW AT THE BALL FIELD

.................

'm hearing cannon fire, unbelievable every time it stops, as I stare wildly out my upstairs window into the cool air and the violet light. But there it is again: the noise of cannon fire at the time of day cannons would have been lit to announce that "we are up, and we are coming. This is your only warning."

A hundred and fifty years erased, I picture boys in trenches waking up fast, with terror or gritty determination or both. A *boom* that feels as if it's reached into your house and shoved you, meanly, to get your attention. It booms off the stone of the mountain, echoing through that cool violet air, the carrying quality of which, like the sound itself, hasn't changed in a hundred years. I'm hearing exactly what the boys heard, what the mothers miles around any battlefield heard from their beds, waiting on sons in trenches.

But it's only some riled-up volunteer fireman on the morning of Wellsville's Founders' Day, with a cannon loaded onto his flatbed truck, driving around setting it off, over and over again. Near the tabernacle in the town square, the other volunteer firefighters are preparing pancakes, and if they're up, I guess, why shouldn't we all be? The town loves it. The town loves that this ritual is so odd, and idiosyncratic, and inconvenient. How often, when else, where, would most people get a chance to hear this? Watching the flash from the mouth of the cannon that I can occasionally see through the trees as this anonymous (to me) man winds his way around Wellsville at 5:00 a.m. is not only surreally silly but also a hushed moment in my year. I remember in a glut of imperialist nostalgia the true hardship of settling not just this contested land but all lands, wrested from someone, surely, but got.

Let me say for the record, my slight ancestry of Native American blood, both Cherokee and Choctaw, inspires the same nearly tearful state when faced with the Trail of Tears. But at this 5:00 a.m., on this morning, I don't justify or overthink my response. I just know for a moment I am in a continuum of history, in a way I find harder to muster up in the pandemonium of out-loud daylight life.

Of course, that's only the first half hour of Founders' Day.

The family who lives next door to our house has four kids, as best we can tell. One is gone on a church mission, or married and moved away, or those are two different kids. The other three, ranging between seventeen and twenty-four, are like bounding cheerful golden retrievers, circling us whenever we appear in public, attracted to our newness. They invite us over to their place for meals, video games, chats in the garage over the bench where their mother cuts wood to build tables and fences. Their mother shames us with her industriousness, but cheerfully.

We also see the kids in town at the White Owl Tavern where they are not supposed to be. They are as cheerful and open then, the guileless sheepishness their mother has instilled in them as apparent on their faces as innocence.

On days like this at festivals right in Wellsville they are like a brigade around us, their enthusiasm sweeping us together into crowds of locals, onto the driveways and lawn chairs of surrounding families. "I'm thinking about getting a tattoo," the younger boy says, eyeing Christopher's arms.

"Oh, no, no, you're not," Chris says. "Your mother will be really mad at me."

"Maybe I'll get a motorcycle," the boy continues, having hovered over Chris's in our own garage. Christopher sighs and shakes his head. But we can't help laughing, and neither can they. Real trouble seems deceptively far away here in the sun on a town green straight out of a Norman Rockwell, blooming with extended families, the flower of fat babies at their centers.

A few hours later, we all gather on Main Street for the parade. Main Street was hopping for about sixty or seventy years, but now it's pretty slow. There's the post office (initially run by the Maughan family, the same that settled the town), the City Hall (which begs to be put in ironic quotation marks), a general store (perpetually for sale since the convenience mart slash Burger King went in at the highway), and Katie's Hair Hut.

I've seen pictures of what Main Street was in the '70s, and by that I mean the 1870s. It was full. The Brenchley Brothers ran a blacksmith shop there, the street in front kept full by horse-drawn wagons waiting for repairs, by men standing around chewing the fat; there was a Wellsville Bank at the corner. Now only a closed car repair shop stands spit-cleaned on the far corner, like a movie set, a testament to the man who ran it in the '50s. The 1950s. This has become a bedroom community, something even I, a brand-new resident, don't want to admit.

So, the parade works its way past the few sleepy storefronts left on Main Street. Teenagers who definitely slept through the cannon fire trot by on painted horses — not paint horses, the type, but painted horses, with war paint on them. Observers know which teenagers are supposed to be Indians because they are bright red; like barn red, Red Delicious apple red. As well, the "squaws," as they themselves insist on being called, tucked behind their boyfriends on each patient horse's back, are Norman Rockwell, Mormon-bred, blond and blue-eyed. No one seems to notice how deeply weird and potentially insulting this all is. Mostly the occasion functions as a moment for the girls to wear cute suede halter tops (branding themselves by the show of skin as non-Mormons, or at least as bad ones) and for the young boys to take off their shirts and holler war cries, without being told to stop.

The neighbor kids with whom we are standing wave at the passing teenagers, and laugh and elbow each other at signals we don't see, in the time-honored tradition of kids everywhere.

After the parade is the Sham Battle. Against a backdrop of the mountain that protects all of Wellsville's west flank, the whole town stands around the baseball field of the grade school while a handful of old men set up the speaker system. In the center of the field stands a circle of covered wagons. Nobody blinks an eye as the mock battle starts with a voice-over on the loud speaker telling the sacred tale of the way in which settlers of the valley would enact mock battles. Even if that were true, I think, and actually I think it isn't, but if it were, well, it was not like this. I watch the bright red girls screw down their braid/headband combos as they gird for battle, watch the boys and grown men tuck their velour loincloths more securely into the band of their Wranglers.

Mostly no one is listening anyway, raptly attentive to the growing preset fire in the center of the wagons, and the slowly tightening grip of teenagers in red face, loping horses in ever more concentric circles inches in front of babies set down on second base. Before too long, the boys are swinging off their horses like trick riders, grappling with anybody in a bonnet or suspenders from the center of the circle. Everyone except the prissiest of the settler brides ends up on the ground in a ring of fire, ripping shirts off men and yelling nonsyllabic nonsense at the womenfolk.

Still in my first year among Mormons, I was surprised to hear a woman behind me in the crowd sigh in disappointment and say to the person beside her, "This was way better last year when they were all drunk."

Or did she say "drunker"?

# WINTER

................

I stand at the fence in my yard watching the horses. It turns out that if you have an empty paddock, and you make eye contact with anyone near here ever, you will soon have horses in your paddock on the premise that you "need it grazed." Especially if the grass has become so long that it pokes lushly, wastefully, through the snows of a hard Rocky Mountain winter.

The air is so cold that the hair in my nostrils is frozen. I smell ice and gray clouds.

I have pulled my longest down coat on, and my tall boots, and if anyone were to look closely under those, I am in my pajamas. This is my uniform for being around my place. I have very quickly thrown off the studied and expensive disheveled styles so popular in Los Angeles in favor of actually disheveled. It's not the most popular look in Cache Valley for ladies — that would be "ladylike" — but I'm rather fully embracing the farm esthetic of muddy barn boots. Whenever I have fed the goats or the horses while wearing bracelets or skirts on my way out to town, the animals seem to barely recognize my scent or motion. I spend a lot of time just standing around my yard or paddock or barn in pajamas; the neighbors who happen to drive by during my strolls and chores have stopped ignoring me in my state of disrepair and started waving hello.

I lean on the fence but make sure not to touch any bare skin to the metal. Whenever it snows more than a couple of inches, I now get into the backyard as quickly as possible because I know the horses will be insane for it. Today is no exception. They race in circles and then skid near me, eyeing me sideways as they lean their bodies onto the fence for me to scratch. Then they jerk away and bite each other, and throw themselves onto the ground and roll. They run again for the sheer joy of it all.

The goat stands near me inside her pen, which abuts the paddock. She shouts at me for hay. She rushes to the top of her doghouse shelter and leaps to the ground for attention, snow puffing into arcs at her landing, and then she butts the fence at the dogs.

The dogs bark at the horses from their safer side of the fence with me, and snarl at the goat. The shorter dogs are nearly covered in snow. It feels like we are all barking with joy at one another.

Everybody's freezing but nobody wants to go inside.

Snowmobiles buzz by on the side road. The man from down the block shushes by with his horses in harness, pulling a chariot. Not a cart or sled, but a chariot. I don't give them so much as a hard stare as I wave at him. This is what we all do when it snows hard. I've seen that chariot a lot.

Tonight there will be tiny moving lights on the side of the mountain, the headlights of snowmobiles curving through the fallow fields and then up the deer and cattle trails. We'll have the smell of our wood-burning fireplace mingling with others' smoke, if Tom down at the repair shop (Why Tom? We don't know.) has given us all the okay to burn, depending on the inversion conditions in the valley. We may or may not have to dig somebody's car out of the snow on the rarely plowed dirt road beside us, but we don't mind.

Have I mentioned I love snow?

# SUDDENLY, WHAT YOU DO
# IS WHAT YOU DO

. . . . . . . . . . . . . . . .

C hristopher started off charmed, when we moved to the valley, that he could do the blue-collar work he'd always loved and was so good at before he'd moved to Los Angeles, now that he was back in the rural setting that seemed to demand this work. He shook off L.A. like a change of clothes. He snapped up his Carhartt insulated coveralls every day that first winter and went off to weld pieces of towers together in the freezing cold.

In Los Angeles, this was a forty-dollar-an-hour job. But here, even with as many white-collar jobs as there were now in the valley, there was still no end of farm boys who'd been welding horse fence, barn gates, and irrigation pipes since they could hold a torch and dodge the flame. Getting good work here was not going to be easy.

By spring, he was a smoker again. He'd quit in L.A., and the man I married was the guy who would come home at midnight from running miles through the streets of Hancock Park, gleaming and healthy. But a winter of standing in the Rocky Mountain cold with greasy hands, surrounded by a few other guys who couldn't get other work, friends of the boss who were drinking on the job and then welding weight-bearing structures, was wearing him down. He wasn't adjusting the way he thought he would. He wasn't, it turned out, loving it like I was. I was stunned.

He loved the fly-fishing. He loved the motorcycling. He loved the horses and the chickens and the goats and the fact that you couldn't get away from our spectacular view of the Rocky Mountains, filling every window, if you tried. He even liked being a pretty obvious fish in a fairly modest pond: he was tattooed, wore his head shaved or greased his early-gray hair back like a fifties movie star, which made him look like the most intimidating gas station attendant you've ever seen in a black-and-white movie; he wore beat-up clothes; he was loud. He stuck out, and he didn't mind that. I had a much more complicated sense of my own position there. I could fit in or stick out, literally according to my outfits. It felt surreal. Rock band T-shirt, stick out. Cardigan (not secondhand), fit in. Knee-length skirt, fit in. Tank top, stick out. It wasn't such a game for him.

Through a new friend named John, an ornithologist, Christopher found out about a job counting bird's nests on the Utah-Wyoming border. Yes, that's a job. He had no other prospects, and he was willing to live a few months in a trailer in the tiny town of Randolph, Utah.

All over the western states, hippies and scientists and hippie scientists take summer jobs tracking the life of the land. They are looking for rare species, or the effects of cattle or sheep grazing on public land, or the efficacy of birth control on wolves, or the health of rivers. They are temporary weird pockets of dissonance, crashing the local senior center's yoga classes, eating all the chips at bingo nights in VFW halls, surprising ranchers and retirees who are not amused. At an informational get-to-know-you meeting in Randolph as the study began, an old rancher approached Christopher. "Son, you can walk on my land," he murmured, clasping Chris's hand. "Just don't find anything endangered."

He didn't. He found hundreds and hundreds of nests, watched dozens of eggs hatch, noted the predation rates of chicks by coyotes, and learned how very far a shrub-steppe bird, a vanna sparrow, or a vesper sparrow, can throw her voice, pitching her sound away from her fragile nest. I camped up on the plateaus with him some nights, and he just rose in the morning and started walking, tapping sage bushes and tumbleweeds with a long stick, wandering off to work from the back of the truck. At night, it was the darkest place I'd ever been in my life.

It was pretty damn good, as summers go, but it wasn't making him happy. He knew now he didn't actually want to become an ornithologist, or a river riparian area specialist, another thought he'd had but one that would also involve science and patience. More worrisome for me, he doubted he could live for long in such a desolate place, where the sun breaking over the mountain straight into the flat darkness of open fields made the meaning of "dawn" abundantly clear. But I craved seeing that truly pitch-black night again, no porch lights, no headlights, no jets, from the moment I felt it close in on me the first time: the delirious loss of equilibrium in not knowing how far that far was unless the moon was full, the rare opposite of sensory overload, the meditative quality of near sensory deprivation.

I didn't even mind the suspicion of the cowboys each day, the first real ones I'd ever seen, as long as they'd just keep letting me sit in the diner with them and eat fries and eggs and try not to stare too long. Every time I visited Randolph, sheep or cows greeted me on the main road in town, nudged begrudgingly away from my car by cowboys on horses, who looked down into my car as they rode on the street, the way long-distance truckers often idly gaze into cars near them on a highway. I stared back at their sweaty silk neckerchiefs, their chaps, their stained hats, the spurs on their boots at my eye level. One late afternoon, I accidentally ordered the last hamburger at the only local restaurant and the whole room went quiet. The cowboy behind me was the same one Christopher had seen forty miles away that morning in a high desert field moving cattle; he'd ridden back to town all day for that hamburger. I did not get the hamburger.

We liked it up there. But as with the other jobs, it turned out Christopher was not going to start riding horses over the backcountry gathering cattle anytime soon, unless they could make a cozier saddle with a sunshade and the Internet on it, and pay more, and make it nearer to more people. I could drag my feet, in the name of research, but Christopher had to make a choice.

So Christopher went back to grad school too. God help me: for acting.

He was the only actor at the university who'd done a shrubsteppe bird study, that's for certain. He'd been a roofer, a welder, a set builder, a mover, and, it's true, an actor as an undergrad. But years of manual labor had distanced him from that tender young boy.

So now we were a writer and an actor. In Utah, not exactly the throbbing heart of artistic industry. Mostly, we lied by omission to our neighbors about our goals. We're teachers, we'd say, because we were also teaching at school. That's our story. We're sticking to it.

But seeds were sown then that I'd have to pay more attention to later. Jobs that would allow us to stay here in this valley indefinitely? Adjunct teacher, veterinarian, nurse, gas station attendant, bookstore clerk, waiter, bank teller, farrier, factory worker at the local La-Z-Boy chair company or Pepperidge Farms. Writer? Maybe. Actor? No.

Still, it wasn't a sure thing. We weren't sure, either of us, what we wanted to *do*.

# TABLE OF CONTENTS

.................

I n a 1973 interview with a young Utah State University student, Mrs. Annie Leishman of Wellsville, Utah, recounted her life. The table of contents is cryptic poetry, a gone-in-a-blink one hundred years, words with the smell of wheat, the splash of an illicit swim in an irrigation ditch, the depth and breadth of experience that passes with each person's passing.

Annie Leishman's Table of Contents: Road Conditions, Description of Church, Dairy Farm, Dairies, Recreation, Thrashing Grain, Irrigation, Electricity, School, Road Improvements, Store on Wheels, Indians and Gypsies, Experiences with Gypsies, Experiences with Indians, Coyotes, Railroads, Shipping Cattle and Hogs, Saw First Car, Chores, Flu Epidemic, Story About Alfalfa Seed, Beets, Typhoid Fever.

# PROCESS

......................

Christopher stands in the snow with our neighbor Bill, staring into the goat pen, cigarettes hanging off their lips, hands jammed in their pockets. "Wanna see something?" Chris calls out as I stumble from the truck, through snow, ice, and rock salt, winding around the three-legged cat that's winding around me. I imagine, not longingly, how sunny it is at our old Spanish-style red-roofed house in Los Angeles. The dogs bark from inside, a tinny noise echoing through the freezing glass and off the snow. The horses are watching, heads low, looking through the fence.

I know the tone of voice my husband is using, the falsely laconic and understated one that means gleeful you-won't-believe-this. I drop my bag and start running for the house yard. I run right up to the dog house that sits inside the pen and peer inside. Sure enough, there's two goats in there. This morning there was only one non-pregnant one.

"Didn't Mandilyn say this goat could no way be pregnant? Yesterday?" I ask without looking away, picturing the assurance with which our new friend here had shaken her head, hands wrapped around the belly of the goat.

"Yeah, well. Their goats are so fat, I guess it seemed impossible. Well, she's right, it does seem impossible."

We all look at the baby a long time. It is curled in a tiny C against its mother, who is smelling it. Bill eventually, slowly, as he does everything, says two things. One, it should be nursing by now and it's not. And two, the sister of this mother goat gave birth only a week ago, in the wrong season as well, and that baby died. It takes me about one second to start dragging everything that moves out of the laundry room. Then it is a stall. It will take a full year for it to stop smelling like one, but I don't know that right now. (And never mind that we have real stalls out back in the barn . . . too far, too cold.) Bill shakes his head but it's not like he's surprised. He already thinks I'm crazy — I did move here from California, after all, something I do not brag about — crazy that I get happy about snow and the way the mountain looks and cattle loose in my front yard. "I want to die and come back as one of your animals," he says sarcastically, but he's already lifting the mother goat, which screams like a child the whole way inside. I picture Bill riding the range moving huge herds of cattle, cowboying until he started having kids ten years ago. The screams do not faze him in the slightest.

The baby fits into my cupped hands. Later when he's bigger I'll hold him down at the vet's while she digs around inside him, searching for his undropped testicle while he yells at us, earsplitting pain. I will have to sit down very fast, betraying my lack of ranch wherewithal, but I will try to maintain some coolness by not actually leaving the room. My husband will stare me in the face as he continues to grip the goat, trying not to do the same thing. Leaving us sweaty and sick, the baby goat will then virtually bounce off the vet's table and then begin to nose sweetly around the office for food, calm as the eye of a storm.

For now, he can't even eat.

Hours later, Bill gone — our country information expert;

we can't believe we've been left alone with this life-or-death moment — Christopher and I stand ankle deep in straw inside our house. Granted, it's the small, enclosed porch off the back, but still, it's carpeted, and looking up to see my clean clothes, glass plates on a shelf, the lamp shining from the kitchen, seems just silly. I hold a phone between my ear and my neck, listening to my friend Mandilyn read from a book: the baby must eat within the night. If it doesn't, it will miss all the colostrum from its mother's milk, along with the imprint of the learning how to nurse, and poof, we will have failed him. I picture myself driving to the ranch and farm supply, buying nipples and supplements and who knows what else (we don't), and setting the clock alarm for every two hours, all for an uncertain result, and I'm tired before I've even begun.

Christopher pins the mother goat, Buddy, against the wall and holds her nearside leg up out of the way. I hold the kid, a one-handed job at this size, but am trying to milk Buddy with my other hand. I hang up the phone with promises to update Mandilyn later (in fact, she and her whole family will drive over, irresistibly drawn by cuteness in a match with death). I hold the kid's chin, his blindness, steering his mouth toward Buddy's moving milk factory. She isn't being willful; she's never done this before either. When the baby (named suddenly Dude, which apparently is what we yell when trying not to swear — because after all, we're in front of a baby) butts his head under Buddy a few times, we know we are in the final stretch. They figure it out.

We are a long way from Hollywood. It had seemed when we lived there like the center of the universe. Friends whom we told we were leaving looked at us as if we'd bought passage into space.

. . .

I know I have fundamentally changed, come a long way from the death of Bambi's mother being an animated dream, a long way from the mores and daily life of my past, when I watch a man open up a bird with his bare hands. It takes both seeing it and living with it to understand that I don't feel horror at the image of it, after it has had time to fossilize into part of my experience. Instead I feel an instant, incisive connection to process, to cycles, to nature's absolute dominion over man, because nature doesn't care about this one bird, whether we do or not. Nature has thousands of birds just in the field where we stand, where our friend just pulled apart this bird with the knowledgeable precision of an ornithologist, which he is. After watching him walk through the gold field of sharp drying safflowers with his rifle cracked open and cocked over his shoulder, after watching his dog careen through the high grass, in synchronicity with the trained falcon flying above, after seeing the dog from the ground and the falcon from the air look at each other to communicate their plan, I just let go of whatever defunct morality I was trying to apply to the situation and know I am in the presence of a process I am not qualified to assess.

I feel no moral panic in watching the dog bring the pheasant to us with his head high and his tail frantically waving in joy, watching any creature do what it does best. Our friend kneels to take the bird from the dog's mouth and holds it loosely in his hand while we watch the small bird close its eyes and die. The falcon watches from a few feet away, near the panting mouth of the dog. In the time it takes for John to tell us what he's about to do, he's done it — tosses the head of the bird to the dog and the body to the falcon.

The falcon messes with the body of the bird briefly, until John takes it back before she can ravage it beyond its usefulness to him. He opens up the small body from the hole she's begun. He pulls out the heart and hands it to her. His hands are covered in blood past the wrists, and all I can think is, "I see. I see." But what I "saw" would take more time to process than that moment allowed.

People who have been hunting all their lives with no compunction to consider the exchange they make and the gravity of the trade, I don't know where to put them. I just remind myself there are too many mule deer for the earth to handle, and before my inner dialogue says we took their space, not the other way around, I try to change the channel.

So I would not like to imply that taking an animal's life, or being present for it, should become easy, some rite-of-passage marker of having arrived at cohesiveness with nature, or authentic rural life, or true Western-ness. Still, it is surely true of all animals, and all conscious people, that the pain we inflict on each other is in some ways due process for living in the world.

# THE MAGIC TRICK

................

**M**onths pass quickly. Late last summer as my first fall semester started, I'd been standing in the corner of a hallway in the university English department building whispering (in tears, let's be honest) into my phone: "I'm too old for this. I can't even work the computer, because it's not like mine, and they keep telling me what to do but I still can't understand, and I haven't been in a classroom in ten years, so do students bring computers to class now?" On my first day, another grad student got a hold of me and asked, "Do you know what your thesis is about? Mine's about Willa Cather's serialization and the dissemination of information back east via periodicals." It was a month before I realized no one else but that guy knew what they were doing either.

And then Founders' Day and then a fall full of fog, which apparently drove the Utes to the top of the nearby mountains for the season back in the day, dying for sun, and then Christmas in these shockingly beautiful mountains and then muddy, fast-water, snow-filled spring.

In the midst of our disbelief at the herds of children here, the high numbers of siblings in so many Mormon families, gentle jokes about what's in the water, I am pregnant.

But of course it wasn't a magic mineral in the water.

I'd stopped taking my birth control pills.

No, I didn't tell him. Yes, I knew what I was doing. For nearly a year, I had used those little ovulation predictor kits from the supermarket, and they worked like a charm: two pink lines, fertile. One pink line, not fertile right this minute. One month, in retrospect, God and percentages and ambivalence and nature won and there I was standing at the fridge thinking, "I'm dying for something vinegary."

You will think this is not fair. Perhaps particularly if you are a man. But you did not live in our various homes with us, two people within four walls for years and years and years. I can say with certainty, and perhaps if you are a woman, or perhaps only the luckiest of women, you can attest to a version of this certainty too: I was in a position to make this choice for both of us, he and I, the decision at least to be ambivalent and to play that roulette. To not make the choice to not get pregnant. I knew we'd be okay no matter what happened, and maybe I knew well enough to even hope.

Christopher takes a deep breath when I tell him, and puts down his wrench and a motorcycle carburetor for what surely in that moment must feel like it will be the last time.

"All right," he says, grinning.

It turns out that theoretically imagining having a baby without any particular aim to do so and being pregnant are two very completely different universes. His growing excitement and my belated fear make us about even in the getting ready department. I have made a lot of unadvised choices in my life, and he's been the one who talked me through the consequences of half of them, and in this way, decisions become alchemically joint.

Previously, we have each moved to California away from our families, alone and without jobs. We then uprooted after ten years of making friends and finding work in order to move somewhere we know nothing about. I have started graduate school after ten years of being out of college. We got married *and* bought our first house *and* moved states *and* started graduate school within the same three weeks, none of these being processes that are light on the planning or paperwork. I married a person I suspected to be an actor. I do not even include here the type of day-to-day choices we both constantly make down the path of most resistance.

But this, this is brave.

Christopher secretly prays for a girl and I secretly pray for a boy.

I know what it is to be a girl. It's so scary in that skin, I wouldn't wish it on anyone. I have no idea what tools I might offer a girl kid, what reactions I might have to any of her troubles other than fiercely stonewalling or actively punching anyone who hurts her, and crying with her when she cries. None of these sounds universally appropriate. I do not, in other words, know yet what, if anything, I might know about myself that's useful.

On the other hand, life seems to be working out. This part, this part I'm living now, is a good part.

# GROUNDWORK

.................

**W**e are accorded some kind of Peter Pan status due to our apparent lack of maturity — we sure enough look like adults, but we don't have children. We don't even have "real" jobs because we're grad students at the local university; we don't even have jobs in our pasts that can be explained without invoking full disbelief. ("You did *what* for television?" As reviewed, I got snacks, for which I got paid an amount that begins to defy even my own belief; Christopher built sets, which he always managed to "overengineer," as he never got the hang of building things for temporary use.) Plus I keep wearing the wrong outfits for a woman my age in this place, not to mention my pajamas out in the yard. So, awkwardly, Christopher and I sit on our horses in the middle of the town arena while Bill trains the 4H kids. Ten-year-olds whiz past me at full gallop. I reassure myself that at least Christopher is more worried than I am; I have more experience on horses than he does, but Bill can't seem to believe that, and keeps demanding that Christopher do more complicated things, faster.

Bill's son Kyle circles near us, looking at our faces. "Most adults in town don't really get my dad," he blurts out, I guess dying to hear what we'll say but fearing an answer. He's using us, I think, as a barometer, the only one available from the outside world, the first people he's been comfortable talking to who aren't from this valley or very near it. He's never been farther than Salt Lake. When we tell him about Bruce Springsteen and Mick Jagger, he doesn't know who we mean. This isn't representative of everyone in the area, not even close, but it is of more than you'd think. He still says "afeared": when he'd recently been assigned to a church mission in Seattle, we were sitting in their kitchen, and Bill said only, "It's really green there. All year." Kyle, then, was afraid of how far that must be, to be so different from here.

"Kyle, what are you talking about?" I'm forced to ask.

"Dad's awkward talking to folks, I guess," Kyle shrugs.

When we'd just moved here, Kyle was awarded his medal for finishing the entire gamut of Boy Scout life, a rite of passage we thought had fallen out in the 1960s. We were invited to the church for the ceremony that would acknowledge him along with five other young men. We were greeted with a lot of hand shaking by those we knew as neighbors, and no curiosity at all by those we didn't. On a table at the back of the room stood projects Kyle had made toward this medal; a photograph that I took of one of his horses pounding through the first snow of this winter stood in an elaborately worked leather frame made by Kyle.

We'd gone back to Kyle's house, where his mother, Gail, made the kind of food she used to cook for cowboys when she hired out at ranches. Sloppy Joes. Trays of potato gratin made from boxes. Even I could see the tension between most of her guests' middle-class expectations and this family's cowboy practicality. I was dying to rip open the curtains, which she keeps closed to keep the room cool; she was too preoccupied to see how odd it was to have visitors sitting in the dark of the living room on this sunny Sunday. Some of us moved outside, where we balanced paper plates on our knees and watched the dog chase the cat through the pasture, watched Bill sneak out behind the round pen to smoke and stare at his horse while the church people talked about the weather.

"Is Kyle excited to go on his mission soon?" I'd asked Bill, for lack of anything else to say, after I finally submitted to temptation and busted permanently out of the dim room for the light. I just wanted to be back by the dusty horses, and out from the awkward chatter of people who were trying so lovingly to be polite to me, when we just didn't have that much to say. We all mean well, but when I am tired, our different churches, different work circles, different pasts, feel not so important to surmount, not every day. I didn't know what to say out here by the paddock either, but the mountain was out here, so I preferred it.

Bill kept leaning on the round pen, leaning on his arm looking in as if seeing a horse circle there, even though it was empty. His forehead was pale where the hat covered it almost all the time except church.

"Sure. Don't know what to do after though." I knew he meant Kyle, because Bill wouldn't tell me if he himself didn't know what to do.

"Is he going to work around here in the valley?"

"Sure. Maybe train some horses with me."

"That's good," I said, but with kind of a question.

"Sure," he said.

He looked back toward the house. "Dog!" he yelled, at his dog, as the dog tried to sidle away up to the reservoir to lick old fish.

I had no idea what Bill thought of Kyle's leaving, what might or might not change, what Kyle wanted, what might be bad news in this scenario or good. I just knew he'd come back to the valley. And that was good, wasn't it?

Kyle wandered back. He was wearing missionary clothing,

church clothes, instead of his usual jeans and snap-front shirt. He yanked at his tie as if I'd mentioned it out loud, pulled his white shirt looser in the back without quite untucking it. He leaned on the pen too.

We all just stood there. I was still not used to standing around like that, not talking.

"How's your party?" I asked him after I waited as long as I could in the silence.

Kyle looked at his dad to see how they felt about the group in there. Bill just flicked away a cigarette without looking up. Kyle shook his head like that was an answer, and clicked his mouth.

I understood this to mean, "They mean well. But that's not my thing in there."

Partially in an effort to stand quietly with the men, also because I never tired of the view, I looked over their round pen at my own house two paddocks away. People waved to us back there as they left the house up front, as the line of cars down the side of the gravel road diminished like a film played backward, and then we were just standing around behind our houses like always.

But today we all three watch his dad circle the arena on his horse, instructing a dozen small kids as he passes each, weaving easily through their figure-eights and spurts and stops and lopes and walks.

"Christopher, you want to go for a lope with a lead change?" Bill calls out.

"No," Christopher calls back.

Bill is the kind of rider who can cut cattle without losing his cigarette. For a while there, to my mind, he's like the Marlboro man I can't help invoking, except with a few broken teeth he can't afford to fix, a secondhand work hat, a tired wife, four children, a job at the railroad.

We sit on horses made skittish by our own nerves, earthbound in a dirt ring full of preteens, while Bill communicates only intention and joy to his horse, and they fly.

Back in my own pasture that week Shorty the horse circles me, ostensibly directed by my hold on the opposite end of the lead rope connected to her headstall. The horse and I both know this is bullshit. She is totally running the show.

Except that, dangerously, neither of us knows very well what we're doing. I know how to *ride* a horse, learning in Los Angeles at an expense that makes my new neighbors laugh horrified at what urban people will do, what with all the horses running around needing a ride at their places. But I've never learned to do ground work with a horse, something seemingly reserved in my past for the mysterious folks who trained us skittish bourgeoisie. It would be one thing if Shorty knew how to lunge herself, rolling a bored and indulgent eye at me from time to time spinning in the center. But no. She is young, and perhaps I am too old. She has a great spirit, and a tender nature, but perhaps someone (Bill) should have let me buy the good old gelding I actually wanted, the horse who would train me instead of the other way around. I must have accidentally conveyed some confidence I absolutely do not have, or nodded too hard at the wrong moment. Whatever the case, I own this horse. She is the prettiest and most expensive lawn ornament I have ever had.

It's true that Christopher and I both enjoy feeding her, along with the other horses we keep from time to time for neighbors and friends, other horses we also do not ride. Even after bludgeoning the ice off the water trough this winter, Christopher comes through the yard with a bit of a swagger on the bitter walk to his truck. It is not the worst way to wake up. Nor, surprisingly, is it the worst thing to happen when you are wakened in the middle of the night by the knowledge, nearly psychic, that your horse has just got out of the fence and is now standing companionably at another fence with the horses down the way. It is less fun when you are alone without gloves in the dark and pregnant and it is zero degrees and icy and the only available help is the teenager next door, whom you must wake up by pounding on his family's door at 3 a.m. But even that is pretty funny in retrospect, especially the memory of the sweet teenager you know whispering his angry sleep-over friend into silence, the one who stands in the middle of the street sullenly looking on, wishing he were back in his sleeping bag on the floor next door. Or perhaps back in town.

As I turn on my heel holding the rope, Bill yells at me just the way he does at his own kids when I do something wrong, and I change the position of my hands, head, or body until the yelling stops.

"Liz!" he shouts. "Hand up!" Over the pumping of my heart, I hear him, and I try to listen while simultaneously moving my feet, in a shifting circle, in such a way as to not fall over myself, yanking the rope down as I go, turning the horse on a dime inexorably toward me. "Liz! Hand forward!" I am fast realizing the difference between hearing and listening.

"*There* you go," he shouts, soothingly, if that's possible. It sounds like balm to me.

"Right!" I call back. "I just — "

"Concentrate!" he shouts. So I do.

It's the last time for a while Bill will help me work with the horse, because after today I'll tell him I'm pregnant and he will not be a party to that foolishness, us standing in the paddock together, my young horse, my blooming responsibility, and me.

I try hard not to picture the horse turning in toward me in confusion, even though I guess I know she'd almost certainly slow to a walk to do so. Eventually, I wear her out enough to get on her. We gallop around the back paddock again and again in a circle—this I know how to do—and even Bill laughs at all the grinning. I don't know why I'm not scared of this, feeling only a slow-down in the middle of a quick storm, the dirt a blur below me, sitting on the spot in a tornado where it's still and sounds only like the blood rushing in my ears.

Especially when I know, because I've watched her do it, that Shorty stomps her hooves at the chickens I got, trying adamantly to kill them.

# GARDENING

..................

**B**ill is moody. He is literally, empirically, actually, the first cowboy I have ever met up close, and so I pay close attention to him. The day we moved in, a neighbor chatting with us in the yard had waved his truck to a stop, and out climbed Bill and his two sons, all of them filthy and smelling mysteriously bad, a smell that turned out to be horse piss and hooves' shavings.

So they didn't want to stop, but they did, and stood ducking and averting their eyes until a wave of conversation that didn't include them set them free.

Bill was a good listener, but the only thing he really wanted to talk about was horses. That suited us fine, because there was absolutely nothing else we had in common. Still, he thought we were funny, and he needed our barn as he'd used it with the permission of the previous owner for storing hay. So he hung around, and we hung around him. Our outsider status meant we got along with him, because of his outsider status. We had become outsiders by moving. He became one by staying still. But we are always conscious of being a little careful around him. One day, when I finally have fellow graduate students out to my house in "the country" (they were often unwilling to make the fifteen-minute drive), we stand at my new vegetable garden poking at the worms. Bill drives by, and I'm pleased when he eases his car to a stop in the dirt, just as he would if I were alone. "You don't want them worms in there," he muses. "They eat all the nutrients."

"No," my smart and mouthy friend pipes up (the one who'd scared the pants off me the first day with his Willa Cather talk). "The worms *make* the nutrients. When they eat stuff and die."

We all stand there. Let it go, I pray to both of them.

Bill is wrong about this, I can't imagine how he could be so wrong, but he knows a lot I don't know, because he's done work none of us coddled white-collar people would imagine or consider (shooting starving and damaged calves comes to mind), work that we often rightly or wrongly valorize; my grad school friend has a bright mind, a kind heart, was taught to speak up when he knew a thing, and incidentally was raised on a hippie farm full of chickens and vegetable gardens, and is only out here in the country with me to go fishing at the reservoir, not pick a fight.

If, once Bill drives away, later, another day, either of them ever says to me, "mouthy smart-ass Democrat college kids," or "ignorant superstitious country bumpkin," I will have no camp to sit in. I will sit my uncomfortable ass right on the sharp fence, and not say a word. But in both scenarios, I will feel like fighting.

# THE HISTORY OF OTHER PEOPLE

.................

Houses in Wellsville sell quickly. The grown children of local families are standing by waiting to snap them up, often having moved away to distant Millville (ten miles) or Providence (twelve miles!) or returning from church missions halfway around the world, dying to get back for the companionship, the history, the babysitting. I can simply not imagine living down the block from my parents, sensing the makings of a bad television sitcom in which grown kids sulk like teenagers (that would be me, in this scenario) and bring their laundry to their mothers, and parents sneak vodka tonics and cigarettes inside the privacy of drawn blinds. Of course, that's not what's happening here in Mormon country (right?), and I feel something surprisingly akin to envy while watching women with babies slung on their hips walk down their own driveways and up another a block away, over and over, all day long.

On the other hand, there is me. And others like me. That is to say, "Californians." I am not from California, but apparently if others' reactions here are to be trusted, any contact stains one with the mark of the place, a mark (A behavior? A way of talking? A way of dressing?) that will probably take years to wear off.

The epithet — snidely and loudly spit: "Californians" — is

ubiquitous. Part of me is still waiting to see this mythical creature that apparently takes over whole real estate areas by force,
sneaks into shops and changes price tags ever higher, ruins roads,
drives as if chased by the devil, causes box stores to spring from
dry earth, and mashes wildlife hither and yon. And actually,
I know the appearance of this devil is a real problem in this
valley. I sense the centrality of this issue to everyone here and
rather than steering clear and wide of it, I sneak under the wing
of it, take it on as my own problem too, disingenuously pulling on the sheep's clothing of the language of it: "open space,
preserving farmland, no second Wal-Mart." For all this, I don't
feel like a wolf. I really want what these people want, and I'm
not *from* California, after all. I begin to talk about Los Angeles
as if it's a mistake I made.

The argument against newcomers (including me, of course)
is this: The valley is going to be bursting from its seams soon,
literally full, the ground all taken, and covered by new houses,
huge chain stores, and more houses. But the houses keep selling,
to locals and newcomers alike, and as long as that's happening,
someone will keep building, until they must stop, defeated I
imagine only by the untenable terrain of the closely surrounding mountains. They'll build in a rush, a permanent tidal wave
over the land, a matrix of changes overlaid onto the story of
the earth itself, the buried green glass of Mason jars, the tin
cooking pans, the downed fence wire, the ghostly stone foun-
dations glimpsed through tall grass, the bones of cattle and
horses and humans.

Eventually, no doubt when it is nearly too late, the small historical societies that are now the hobby of elderly ladies, infor-
mal branches of the ladies' Relief Societies in each local church
ward, will get pissed. They'll get organized. They'll come out
of their tabernacle and stake building basement meeting halls,

waving the yellowing paper of brittle family trees, photographs, and Bibles, and demand an end to the ripping down of pioneer houses. Not in time for my house probably, but maybe in time to keep the general character of at least Wellsville intact. In case they don't, though, I'm being careful to remember it the way I found it. I can't even pretend I know fully yet why I feel a personal investment here. And I know I didn't come early to the valley, I'm not blind. I didn't even beat the McDonald's here. But I can hold in my mind my time, this place for a few years, like a photograph or a small slim book, and because it is my story and I get to choose, I can look backward rather than forward. Along with my precious present days, I can remember other people's histories and, weaving tightly, make them part of my own.

# SPRING

..................

The lilac flowers are so monstrous, so biblically lush with the weight of heavy blooms, the kind of blooms that lulled Beauty's father into plucking a rose and losing a daughter, that I have to stand and laugh at the bushes.

California of course is known for its constant state of bloom, the exoticism of birds of paradise and hibiscus and angel's trumpet. But the lilac and hops bushes of grandmothers' backyards are the ones I like, the heirloom pageant queens that make me feel as if I have walked into a Tennessee Williams play, like my date might pick me up in his Studebaker any minute, like I can wipe my hands on the cotton print dress I've been wearing to feed the chickens and be clean enough to eat the mint right off the bush next to the back stoop in the kitchen yard.

This last part is true.

Why are they here, these monsters, and why are they huge? Because the cool season is long for lilacs in the mountains, late April until deep into July, and because just as no one has altered, or "bothered with," our house, no one has trimmed or ripped out these lovely dreams, planted at least forty years ago by a person I'll never know, who would purse their lips in shock at the state of them now.

I just sit on the ground out there in the shade of the newly blooming lilacs — the lilacs throw shade! Ridiculous! — and try and watch my carrot shoots come out of the ground; the garden I dug after the hard winter is on the mountain-view side of the house where it gets full-on sun from noon till dark, because the growing season for veggies will be short. Don't even try peppers, the man says at the seed store. The yellow cat that had wound herself around us from the start follows me away from her food in the garage and lies purring in the sun on the warm turned dirt of the garden bed, gazing at me through slatted eyes.

Of course it will snow in May, and maybe in June, I learned that the very first time I drove here. And I'll be outside in my pajamas and snow boots even as it falls, gingerly shaking the snow's weight off the blooming branches of these bushes. But it's a worthwhile trade-off. Another place or time, I would break off perhaps one small handful of these, float them in water in a tiny china cup, visit them in a windowsill until they faded quickly away. But now I pick armloads, indulgent and ridiculous *armloads* of flowers, jam the branches in tall buckets I can barely walk around in our tiny house. I am rich with lilacs.

# THE BOX C

................

There will be no spa visits, white-water rafting, or antique shopping for used wagon wheels at the dude ranch I am visiting in farthest northwestern Utah. I applied for a grant for summer research and was stunned to win it, the full amount of money, and I immediately decided to blow it in one place. After all, they knew I was studying dude ranches. Still, I feel like I am getting away with something.

When I call to make the reservation, the proprietress tells me I will be staying in the bunkhouse with their summer wrangler, a French kid who had found the place online. Perfect, I think, remembering from past travels the way the French seem to love the idea of the Old West, hoping for my own entertainment that this kid would be decked out in his movie version of a cowboy outfit. I was not jazzed knowing he must smoke — he's French, right? — but figured since I was not telling these people I was pregnant, due to my worries about their judgment or at least their insurance limitations, and since I had to use my grant money this summer or lose it, I'd just have to live with some guilt. The baby still seemed nearly unreal to me anyway, a palm-sized curve of tiredness and hunger.

The town of Grouse Creek pops out of nowhere, though I really hate it when people say that, assuming that anyplace is nowhere because they weren't there ten minutes before they passed this judgment. But after almost a hundred miles seeing ten cars, nearly a hundred seeing none, and about thirty miles of dirt road, a place begins to qualify. When I drive through the town twice, just one lovely curve on a suddenly paved road, without finding the entrance to the Box C Ranch, I know I have to stop to ask directions. I know from my experience in Wellsville that anyone I ask is going to know, and that I am probably welcome at the door of their homes, but I stop at the tiny general store. The woman chatting across the counter, to a man sitting next to a cast-iron stove, says go to the end of town, across from the church. I know without asking what church that would be; the Mormon church at the end of town is surrounded with markers I could now recognize: a new building with an old-fashioned steeple, a playground, people, cars, plaques that indicate its recent history. It looks like people used it; the sweet old Episcopalian churches I grew up with, closed all week and set back into overgrown gardens, are back in the Midwest.

I find not the ranch there, but the family's own house. I sit and eat while the ten-year-old daughter of the family watches me from the couch, inexplicably in a swimsuit until her mother mentions she has skipped practice. Where's practice, I ask. Tremonton, she says. Nearly a hundred miles away. While I sit at the kitchen table, the mother tells me about an accident her husband had recently with a combine, and about the long drive (two hundred miles) to the Salt Lake City hospital while he basically held his face together with his chewed-up hands. I don't ask how his face got that close to the blades, and I continue to eat my chili and cornbread straight through the graphic story. Plastic surgery ensued. By the time the actual man enters the house I expect a monster.

The rancher at Box C is in fact a perfectly normal looking

man, even handsome, who looks as if God had touched his face here and there after it was just about set, pushing things just slightly askew. He nods at me in a friendly way, and declines shaking hands because he's covered in all manner of outdoor dirt. He and I will talk a lot over the next few days, about cattle range practices and piñon pine trees, while other guests hem and haw and giggle at horse farts, all of us on horseback high on mountain ranges in the sun, somewhere over the Idaho state line.

The French kid turns out not to be a smoker. Quiet, dressed in clothes the family had picked out for him straight off the plane before they drove out of Salt Lake, he is a horse person, but not a cowboy. There is a distinction here. Yves had grown up riding English. I picture the hazy day I long ago spent at the beach in Deauville, on the north coast of France, far more Jane Austen than Owen Wister. The family had thought they were hiring a girl — Eve — and were only puzzled at her shoe size, sent ahead by e-mail so they could get riding boots for the new hire. Too polite to clarify based on that one fact, they had found Yves at the airport, slight, dark-haired, reticent but good humored, with no idea what he was in for. "I thought I'd have someone to help clean up and cook for guests," the mother tells me. Yves is a confident, steady rider and guide and more than once notices when I am pissed off at my horse.

The only other guests for the weekend turn out to be world travelers, a fact their mother never lets me forget. When I ask if they are familiar with the area, and what they expect to find, I am rewarded with the tale of "her children, who have camped in places where trees needed to be cut down in order to pass, in the wilds of Wyoming." After a stunned moment in which I only raise my eyebrows, one of the children says apologetically, essentially his mother's translator into the vernacular of the unpretentious: "We were born in Salt Lake."

Still, not exactly good hands with horses. I realize I am the most reserved of the group when asked on the first day if we all have experience on horseback. I know enough to know what all I don't know and it takes them a day to get me to say I have my own horses at home. This visiting family, however, who gave a positive clarion call ("Of course!") when asked, spends the next two days letting their horses leap them over mountain boulders at a run, only to settle nose to butt again, like the spurt of briefly speeding cars on a packed highway in a Los Angeles rush hour.

It is not a comfortable riding style for a pregnant woman, especially a first-timer surprised to feel the first glimmer of protection for the unknowable science experiment she is carrying around. Gripping my reins and gritting my teeth, lurching uphill at a forty-five-degree angle, I find myself furious at the shrieks of glee from the others as we pound on our saddles at a rough trot. Yves nods approvingly when I kick my own horse out of the lineup at a lope and curl out to the side again and again, making room to walk. The two most sublime moments I have: watching the horses being herded out of the mountain fields each morning, a rushing mass of natural instinct flowing down, followed by an old white pickup truck; and watching reruns of the television show *Friends* with Yves in the evenings in the bunkhouse, his favorite show and the only personal event he planned his time around. Each night, Yves and I watch reruns, me idly flipping through church brochures from the coffee table and giggling while he belly-laughs.

"You are from Los Angeles?" he asks.

"Yes," I say, picturing the actors from *Friends* eating lunch at the Warner Bros. commissary, stories I'd heard when Christopher worked nearby on the stage for *E.R.*

Yves's face is a perfect blank, at a loss for where to begin on the subject of a life in Los Angeles.

Yves tells me he hasn't been anywhere this summer but the ranch. Has seen nothing else of America, ever. I imagine the impression he's got. "It's pretty remote," he says in a supreme moment of understatement.

At one of the group dinners, one particularly chummy evening, Yves brings out the very thoughtful, fairly expensive Champagne he'd brought his host family as a gift. I thought for sure someone would have explained the Latter-day Saints religion to him, since I'd seen the pamphlets in the bunkhouse and am sure, if my own neighborhood is any indication of behavior, that they must have at least invited him to church if he was a long-term guest. Still, he looks confused when the family and the visitors, also Mormon by the way, all smile politely and indulgently, say thank you, and set the bottle aside on the table. I try to catch his eye, though I have no idea what I might say there in front of everyone, what gracious but brief explanation I might construct.

Dinner that night is meatballs in red sauce. I've been on a tear since moving to Utah, eating everything set before me with unqualified energy. Food I haven't seen since my grandmother's house in Oklahoma, or since the church coffee hours of my youth, is the norm in Utah. Jell-O salads, meatloaf, broccoli mayo side dishes. The burgers at the rodeo back in Cache Valley are the best I've ever had in my life.

But here is the line I can't cross. I've always disliked sweet red sauce, anything remotely near ketchup, and this one tonight smells like Chef Boyardee to me. I muster one bite. It is the very outermost edge of polite. And with that I am finally, conclusively, pregnant.

"Are you hungry?" Yves asks, a little clumsily bringing attention to my plight.

The world travelers look on, offering nothing by way of deflection.

"Are you all right?" my hostess asks nicely. She deserves an explanation, after all her noodle bakes and pancakes.

"I'm pregnant," I say. "I'm sure this food is good," I say lamely. Sympathy flows back my way. The plate is removed.

I ultimately leave a day early. The lurching about on horseback up mountains contributes but isn't the whole of it. I am tired.

The youngest of the Box C family's children is a girl (the one who'd skipped her swimming lesson), a treasured and hoped-for child, born ten years after her brothers. I wait with her at a creek side in the shade of our grazing horses and a ragged line of cottonwood trees, one long day when she just can't finish a hot trail ride with the others and they have to go and get the trucks and trailers. I have alternately felt such grace as she holds out blade after blade of grass to me, and aggravation as I want her to just stop talking, tired myself from the secret in my belly. But wouldn't I want someone to show only patience to my kid if they were stuck in the shade of their horses together? I am conscious suddenly of the depth of trust my hosts have shown me, leaving me there with their wriggling blond-haired gift.

I've talked a lot to the mother of this family that owns the Box C, and she isn't from Grouse Creek. She'd asked a friend to introduce her to a cowboy; then when they were dating she'd begged him to come to Salt Lake City for a date, to please drive out from Grouse Creek where his family lived and worked. "Well, then, pray for rain," he'd tell her. Years later, there she is, no doubt still praying for rain. When she tries to get her older boys to go to Salt Lake with her for an all-expense-paid weekend on her, dinner in restaurants, movies, shopping, she says they tell her they just want to stay home and do "normal" stuff. Like break horses, herd lost cattle from the crest of the mountains back onto their land, sleep out under the stars, in the middle of "nowhere," on their family's own land.

# STUDENT TEACHING

.................

I teach at the local university while I work toward my master's degree. I am now in my fourth cycle, my fourth semester of teaching local kids. Mostly local anyway, nearly always from Utah, and often enough the first generation to college. My students are overwhelmingly fair-skinned, usually blond, heavy on the Brittanys and Ashleys. They are absolutely the most well-intentioned young adults I've ever met. When I mispronounce one of the most common last names in the valley (sometimes it seems as if everyone has one of perhaps six last names), by calling out "Lishman" for attendance, everyone in the class intones "Leishman" at once.

Apathy is nonexistent. On the other hand, they've been telling me that there isn't much racism in the valley because there isn't much diversity, so the issue doesn't come up. They've been telling me there's a group called Evergreen that fixes gay kids till they're straight. They tell me they've been taught to cross the street if they see a Mexican boy coming because those guys are overly sexual. They whisper the word *feminism*, and use it against each other as an insult. I start to dread teaching the section on cultural awareness because those are the days I go back to my office and cry. For the deep unfairness to all the gay kids, and nonwhite kids, and girls who just want more, that find themselves unlucky enough to be in this valley. For the heavy baggage these seemingly blessed kids are about to carry into the world, cowering at R-rated movies and the gorgeous vibrant life of city sidewalks everywhere else.

They have as long a path out of here as I had in.

# MEMORIAL DAY

..................

This tiny cemetery on a hill, surrounded by spanking new homes, must have been more remote in 1856 when Wellsville was settled. Not a day's wagon ride or anything, but special, set apart, not under anyone's kitchen window as it is to the south edge now. I stand in the back of a small gathered crowd and listen to the names of dead soldiers called out on Memorial Day. As if they stutter, the veterans reading the list repeat most family names not twice but five, eight, or more times, this public list a marker of painful significant generational losses within close-knit extended families. Sons lost to five wars.

I can only nod with my head respectfully down, staring at the patchy grass, smelling the cold wind off the mountain, listening to the voices carrying over from houses across the way, while others pray for their family members. My grandfather, my father, my brothers, none went to war, mostly academics a few years the wrong age one direction or another.

And here I stand in the cemetery of strangers. I've never been to a funeral for anyone in my family. We never lived near enough. And now I've begun to avoid them. Still, no one can avoid a national memory; do we all hear the faint echo of this repeated news during each war — another one lost, and another?

I see the repeating glimmer of a man in a uniform too formal for this little town walking up a short path to the rarely used front door of a farmhouse. I wander off from the back of this solemn group to walk the browning grass between the old stones, no relation to anyone.

A double take at one stone: "He froze to death."

Many, many women lie beside their strings of smaller single stones: a child, a child, a child.

Many men are buried near their multiple and concurrent wives. These soft-edged low-lying stones seem far from capable of generating the initial surprise they gave me when I first arrived — I feel like an old pro now more than a year in, approaching our second summer — and a world away from the titillation that Mark Twain describes in *Roughing It*, of Salt Lake City in the mid- to late nineteenth century: "We felt a curiosity to ask every child how many mothers it had, and if it could tell them apart; and we experienced a thrill every time a dwelling-house door opened and shut as we passed . . . for we so longed to have a good satisfying look at a Mormon family in all its comprehensive ampleness, disposed in the customary concentric rings of its home circle." More than a hundred years later, many people I know in the valley refer to their great- (or great-great-, depending on the age of the speaker) grandmothers' husband's other wives without a blink. Not funny or curious now, these people are simply gone, unaffected in the end by history's judgment either way.

Yet while I walk, slowly, thoughtfully, I am also thinking this, too quickly: "Do you get buried next to your husband? Will I get buried next to my husband? Where? I could be anywhere. What will be my view a hundred years after I'm buried? And then I'll have decided not to be buried next to my parents? Is that bad? And what do they want? Do I have to have a big old box? Can't I just be set in the ground so the critters can get at me?" It's distracting. I try to turn it off. I try to turn it off well before I reach the part where I consider how my kid will live on without me and maybe will tend my grave, and how that makes me so abysmally sad, but that's the good version, the lucky version, out of all the world's myriad possibilities of disaster and joy.

I see the family names of people I know now personally — students I've taught since my move, my neighbors, the women who invite me to each Relief Society meeting (the women's club of the Latter-day Saints) in my neighborhood. I know I may be only a few steps from stones that bear some of these women's own names, centered above a birth date and a dash, followed by an empty space, flashingly blank, hollow and haunting. When we've been together, as the ladies talk about buying and selling houses, moving in and moving away, and who's from where, more than one older woman laughs lightly and contentedly as she tells me: "Oh, I will certainly die here." Oh, I will certainly die here, not written by miners pinned under subterranean rocks, or whispered mournfully by mountain climbers frozen to high peaks with broken legs, is as unknown a feeling to me, as unfamiliar, as eternal life.

The Memorial Day ceremony ends with taps. I am already climbing into my car, trying to beat the crowd, such as it is, that will be maneuvering out of the cemetery soon. We blend seamlessly with the light early lunch "traffic" that carts children and parents to and from the new driveways nearby. Nearly impossible to reconcile this image, the pedestrian and mundane urgency of forgotten grocery lists and soccer shoes, with the faint etchings of full lives on pioneer graves mere steps away, fading away daily like an old unfixed photograph. Yet I have discovered these are nearly to a one the very families that surround me in my daily life even now; the people are all relatives to each other barely separated by a nearly transparent scrim of time.

Time's a-ticking.

# YOKED

.................

G ingerly opening the stove, I throw wood into the small side chamber. When the water boils, I can do dishes. The back porch is less hot than this infernal box of a kitchen, so I stand back there staring at the surface of the water in the pot from across the room. From time to time, I shoot a glance at the woman forking hay up onto the horse-pulled wagon in the field next to me, whenever I hear the music of yoked draft horses, pulling an old iron plow across new fields of wheat, come to a halt.

Occasionally, she shoots a look toward me too — she's in charge of all volunteers — turning her head fully ninety degrees to see past the edge of her bonnet. Can she see me standing still in here? I'm hot, I'm tired. Mostly, however, I wonder in that moment, how do I look?

As a "reenactor" at the American West Heritage Center, a living history museum on the highway outside Wellsville, I wasn't having to do a lot of acting. It was no effort at all to seem authentically hot, frazzled, and put upon. I thought often, usually as I pulled a sullen or overexcited child around on a horse or leaned over a steaming vat of hot water rubbing a dishcloth up and down a board, about my first day at the center. I'd brought my knitting, intending to sit on a rocking chair in my pretty outfit, inside a screen door, listening to bees buzz in the sunny garden, occasionally showing a "guest" around this 1910 farmhouse, about which, incidentally, I can tell you anything, anything you want to know. The Victrola, for instance, was bought in 1921 from a local company. It was a great luxury.

My butt hit that chair once all summer. I spent most of my time feeding chickens, watering and weeding an unmanageably huge garden, catching snotty horses, sweeping floors with inadequate brooms, shooing unkempt and unthankful kittens away from the too-small house, and doing dishes by hand over a steaming tub of water. All chores, I might mention, that I did then daily at my own home and needed to be at home doing.

I didn't hear anyone else at the "1910 house," as we called it, express this feeling. The few older volunteers were largely from our nearby town of Logan and were much more likely to be eating at Olive Garden on their own time than feeding chickens. Most of the volunteers, I was surprised to discover, were about sixteen years old and female. I had pictured museum docents, genteel elderly ladies holding index cards of cramped handwriting, the marginalia of a family's life. Instead, the house was swarming with flush-faced kids, straw hats flung down their backs, tracking hay into the wood-floored kitchen. This was, of course, pretty authentic. And I felt completely genuine exasperation every time the girls were discovered chatting up boys in the barn rather than weeding.

But I understood — they loved the outfits. Playing in these clothes in this setting was a magical draw. It's what we were all doing, really.

A distracted and harried volunteer organizer, on my outfit-getting day, after I'd reviewed a binder of historical information thicker than any of my school texts, walked me into what looked from the outside to be a blacksmith shop but was actually a warren of sheet-rocked white halls leading to rooms filled with filing cabinets and racks of costumes. She wanted to know what would fit, primarily, with no attendant history lesson or sentimentality, tossing aside garments with a murmured "No, that's frontier" — the frontier reenactors' outfits — and tossing toward me anything that looked roughly smallish medium. I, on the other hand, was deeply concerned with authenticity, sure, but more with what fulfilled my own idea of a good turn-of-the-century outfit. I got a decent middy blouse, a lovely long skirt, slim work boots, and black stockings, not the sexy kind. The apron — oh, the apron. I was never happy with it. It was somehow not what I'd pictured. I wanted the kind you hang around your neck like a housedress, having a sense this was more flattering to my figure than the kind I got, which tied around my waist. I giggled that day at my shallowness, but I really did covet the aprons of other lucky reenactors, swinging about them as they swept, every day I worked.

One day, tepees had been moved up to the central paddock. Even I, a rube, could see how jarring that was to the experience of historical reality we were supposed to be trying to re-create. "What's up with that?" I asked a passing blacksmith. "Big weekend for visitors," he said. "And none of them go down to the back field's Native American encampment. It's hard to find way back there, and it's not very wheelchair accessible."

Later, we sat down to lunch behind the settlers' house at picnic tables, all of us in costume, to food cooked by feeding wood to the iron stove, and pickles made from the garden behind it. At the end of the table, there was a Shoshone kid in period native costume.

No one talked to him because no one knew him. He was new. More recent than us at this virtual theme park of Western trivia, on land that withstood the insult of theme-park-ness, land where in a broader sense we — do I even need to spell out this metaphor? — were so much newer than him. Maybe he wasn't talking to us.

How struck I was by the import of his being present to enact this past. How many of us are heirs to so many infinite varieties of nostalgia, or remembrance.

# 3

## THIS IS THE PLACE

·················

# THAT BRIGHT SUMMER

................

I am watching children's childhood memories stack up every day, and most nights. My neighbor Corey, ten years old, doesn't know yet that he will remember riding his horse every day of the summer (through my yard, incidentally) up and down the streets and mountains of Wellsville, but I already know he will. I already know he'll remember being one of the herd of kids that overruns the local fairs and festivals, "helping" park cars, dressed as a really short cowboy, chasing down missed calves in the steer-roping competition, and at least once trying to outrun the lot of them as they turn on him when they'd had enough, publicly shooting him right over the arena fence, at which point he becomes part of other people's memories of this bright summer.

In my brief time here I've already watched Corey move from mutton busting to bull riding. Mutton busting is little kids clinging to the backs of sheep, which are spanked out into the arena from the chutes for about four seconds of glory till the kid slips down, still gripping, to the sheep's belly and lets go for a brief trample by sheep hooves, or gets plucked off by a rodeo clown standing by. It's as good as it sounds.

One late-summer rodeo night at the Wellsville arena, we sit on lawn chairs in the back of our truck, backed up next to the fence. One side of the arena is the chutes, one side is the bleachers, one is folding lawn chairs in the parking lot, and the final side is a line of pickups all backed up to watch the rodeo from the comfort of our own truckbeds. We didn't invent this great idea, of course. We copied the feisty young adult crowd who has adopted us, married Mormons around twenty-five to thirty. One of our neighbors, the kind of woman who grew up from high school cheerleader into sassy-mouthed PTA firecracker, leans on our truck. Her back pasture is the one between ours and Bill's. Her husband and my husband shake hands over the side of the truck.

"Where's Corey?" she asks.

"Too old for this now," I say, because this is what Corey, ten, has told me himself earlier today.

"Pff. Since when, last week?"

"Apparently."

Her husband, a huge ex-cowboy who works at a factory somewhere nearby, says, "Corey's tiny. That kid."

But Corey grew, at least into the "small" bull-riding class of competition, though we'd never shame Corey by pointing out the obvious; the small bulls were still big enough for him to break an arm falling off one, as we found out the next week.

I know about the day he came home crying because kids at school made fun of him for not being into "real" sports, the mark of a community in an uncomfortable transition. Ten years ago, the rodeo team looked like heroes. Now football and baseball have that shine, but as Corey's father, Bill, pointed out, gently, gently, those kids will grow out of their sports and be lost. Corey will have horses for life.

Some of the neighborhood kids ride in our back paddock, now that their parents tentatively accept that we are horse, kid, Mormon, and neighborhood friendly, because our place is a few blocks closer to them than the Wellsville arena at the edge of town. I look up from my writing often to see them out there; their time involves a lot of sitting on the fence in the shade near the house, and I hear their voices more than their horses. One kid at a time rides while the others watch and chat, not because there isn't room for more to ride at once, but because it's really not about riding, is it? One girl who does queening — competes for, and rides as, a junior queen at local rodeos — grows nearly a foot over that first summer. Her hair gets longer, her belt buckles get fancier. She has always talked a mile a minute and that un-self-consciously continues; I've passed Bill, while coaching 4H for them, shaking his head and smiling at her dumbstruck as she tells many an animated story, charmed by the exuberance coming off her in sonic waves.

Many days that I write at home go roughly the same. About 2:00 p.m., I begin to hear the back gate click shut from time to time. By 3:00 p.m., it is clicking open and shut about every ten minutes. Some kid — the junior rodeo queen, or Corey, or others whose names I haven't caught but whose parents I would recognize — will eventually knock on my back kitchen door. All of them, nearly to a one, will be peering at me from under blond hair glowing in the sun. Wearing small boots. Shirts tucked in with big shiny belts. Their skin looks as clean as the day after they were born. As a group, they all kind of sparkle with what to me, from Los Angeles, seems a statistically impossible whiteness. But they all carry the assumption of goodness in the world, the thing that makes them knock on my door when they need anything they can think of and assume the door will open and I will have it.

"Can I use your bathroom?"

"Well, yeah," I say like the mother figure they expect me to be, though for myself I am abruptly conscious of my eccentric writer's writing outfit, some variation of thread-bare T-shirt, sweatpants with all the elastic cut off, and slippers.

As I settle back at my desk, another will knock.

"Can we play with the goats?"

"Well, yeah. Bring the dog in the house first, please."

"Yes, ma'am."

I watch them try to wrangle my dog, which is used to my voice commands and thinks being pulled by the collar by disorganized kids is only an awesome game. The dog and I make eye contact; she is having the time of her life. Still, the kids don't give up.

By now I am tired of sitting at my desk waiting to be interrupted. I crouch with them around the goats' doghouse where the younger goat lies. The kids lean on me un-self-consciously, assuming in me a genetic general motherness that's present in most women they meet around here; inside, I feel utter surprise at the shift I have undertaken from girl about town to someone anyone might rely on.

In five minutes, they are restless. "Can we use your brush and pick?"

"Yes, but put it back in the barn, please." They scatter, like a school of fish, and then flow out the door back together.

The hose goes on, I can hear it through the walls, and the patient horses start to get washed again.

They tell me stories whenever I get too near their orbit at a volatile time of day. I hear about school, who was bad, who left to go hunting with their families but without school permission, whose dad did what. I remember, distantly, the time a homeless man who used to collect recyclables in our Los Angeles neighborhood joined in the conversation of a few neighbors on the corner. "Wow," he sighed, "those folks at 765 really drink *a lot* of wine."

A web, I think. One side of the web twitches, and the whole network of threads moves with it, feels it. My neighbors lose jobs, and get pregnant, and grounded, and I just sit in my backyard and listen for it. I commit to thinking of these times with the kids as a way of engaging, and try to stop thinking of it as interrupting, even when I am called out of the shower to open a tricky gate for a kindergartner yelling from the top of a horse. I begin over time to wear more modest layers and buy better-looking slippers.

So the kids come in to the house for bathroom breaks; I take down the arty photo of a nude that I'd hung in the bathroom and lean it on a shelf in my office. The kids hold the chicks when these are new, let the goats and the dogs out to pet but only after asking politely. They borrow tack and brushes and the hose and leave it all hanging everywhere, but they never, ever forget to latch the gates.

One rainy day I am watching Camille, a girl who has already distinguished herself from the other kids by her sunny, calm smile, by her self-assurance, by her rapt attention when the vet and the farrier visit, by the huge chuckle she can't help but give the other kids when they say something outlandish, when one of them for instance says: "I'm going to marry the best-looking girl in the valley." Tacking up takes a while, plus the ride on her horse from her house to ours takes about ten minutes at a walk, and maybe that's the reason for her determination to ride around our paddock in the soaking rain on this embattling day. But maybe it simply never occurs to her to turn back.

I lean out the kitchen door, hand pushing the screen against the pressure of the rain. I wave to her through the gray air. "You all right out there?"

"Oh yeah," she calls back cheerfully, her voice ushering out from the hanging hood of her jacket. I back into my warm house, snapping the doors shut.

I watch through my window as she unlatches the gate, walks the horse in, and turns carefully to close the wet and slick metal gate-latch behind her. She trudges to the center, lunges the horse as long as he needs, checks his hooves for rocks, gets on carefully in the slipping mud. And she rides that horse in that drenching rain for more than an hour, maybe more than two. I write, peek out the window, write, make a cup of tea. The *dogs* won't even go outside. And she rides and rides and rides.

Camille becomes my child's first babysitter. When the time comes, no one needs to express in so many words her character to me. I get it.

I'd never met a girl like her before, one that was childlike in all the ways you hope she'd stay childlike, and aware and self-assured and conscientious in all the ways you generally wish on kids past ten. But I'd never been around kids raised with the responsibility of 1,500-pound pets. Or with the structure of some serious religion and some deeply entrenched community.

In fact, the more I thought about it, I'd never been much around kids at all.

# GUS

.................

We'd rented a minivan just to get the Great Dane to Utah. Patience itself, he'd curled his lanky frame into a circle and lain down with a sigh for hundreds of miles at a time. This is the dog that cowered from our pair of ten-pound lady dachshunds; who looked at us in surprise when less confident dogs growled at him out of pure preemptive fear, hovering as they did at the level of his shoulder at best. But he never fought. This is Gus: he ate a cake right off the center of the kitchen table the day we brought him home from the rescue, accepting the accidental but wonderful welcome as a sure sign of his beneficent world, no thought clearer on his face than "well, duh," at how able he was to reach so high.

He had lasted a long time. Pumped with glucosamine and love, his joints had lasted years longer than most Great Danes we'd heard about. He was nearly twelve when he finally couldn't do it anymore, couldn't heave his prehistoric-looking frame up off the floor bed on which he slept, not even for a short amble around the pasture to sniff the sage and pee.

Christopher digs a hole in the garden while we wait for the vet to come to us. I watch Chris dig with his whole self, attacking the dirt, stopping to sit down without looking at the house where I sit at the window, pushing his hands off his knees to stand and start again. It's a big, deep hole. Bigger than even it needs to be for a hundred-plus-pound dog. The neighbor boy comes by to offer to help and Christopher turns him down. "How can you do it?" I ask sloppily, ungraciously, through my own tears on his way inside. "Well," he says, "now I know how to deal with a dog's death, or start to. You dig the hole."

An action. A meditation.

The vet's assistant is the same girl who sells me burgers at the rodeo. I lay my hands on the dog, where he lies dreamily on his side; I kiss his bony face and then leave the room. I crouch on the bottom of the stairs in the kitchen. I hold my breath for as long as possible between breaths, listening to the murmuring in the next room between my ragged noise. Christopher stays for the shot, petting Gus.

It's funny. Or maybe I mean ironic, or interesting, or some damn other thing. I'm the one who searches in everything for a lesson, especially as it may relate to death. I'm the one who wants the animals everywhere, underfoot and in the barn and rooting around in the yard, dumbly standing on the road giving me heart attacks. But it's Christopher, in the end, so far, who has the courage to be in the room, to close the animal's eyes, to carry it away. The same spirit that makes Christopher stand under things that are falling if they need to be caught, that pushes cars out of icy ditches when no one else will do it, does this. I don't think it's a special connection to the spiritual that makes this possible for him; I think it's what he perceives must be done. I can't do it, so he does it.

I could aspire to a lot of things: fame, big house, world travel, 360-degree self-awareness, bottomless confidence. But what I really want is simple: to honor the animal, honor the cycle of which I am also a part, to unlock my hands enough, to be there not just for the after but in the moment. I just want to be brave enough to stay in the room.

# CHICKEN LESSONS

..................

This is something I am learning here: life spans, of animals, humans, and objects, become relevant to each other (or perhaps I should say, reveal their relevance), open to connection and examination from all angles. Maybe it was the sea of humanity teeming forward at all times that veiled the quieter ebbing flow when I lived in Los Angeles; besides, not even plants died cyclically there. Here, it seems every birth is balanced by a death: my cat gives birth, but cannot nurse a lost kitten Corey finds in the field nearby and it dies in her bed. I watch new calves, born in the field across from me, slip wetly out after hours of the mother making a racket that seems to always start at night, and then watch them loaded into flatbed trucks and driven away. And then there are the chickens.

Chickens represent a much shorter span of time than one might hope, even at best. I'd stood at the IFA one day, months back, peering into narrow cages stacked three high on a table. Inside was the perfect oxymoron of man-made nature: tiny chicks bred from an intentionally developed bird, which now in its peeping baby form was resistant in smell, sound, and fragility to being deemed useful or intentional in any way. It is like watching a miniature version of an epic saga: battles, deaths, lives, dirty water, diminishing food, factors at work the birds themselves cannot control. The scenario feels a bit Greek in scale until I remind myself I'm standing next a pinging cash register with a rack of candy fruit slices and Maglights.

The chicks themselves look entirely different from their adult counterparts, unprepared for this war, all fuzz and soft feet with nearly translucent claws. I look at the order form beneath the cages.

"How do you tell what sex they are?" I ask the saleswoman who is digging her hands down into the battlefield, scooping up fuzz balls like the fate god of birds. I've noticed that females cost more on the form.

"Well, it's not easy," she says, holding out a bird. We both look at it, and really, the question nearly answers itself. The chick is a cloud of feathers. Much smaller than her palm. Chicken sexers are well trained in making an educated guess, at best. I am undaunted, or as some would say, naïve. I take a catalog home.

Cindy at the IFA calls one early spring morning to tell me my chicks are in, months after the dark winter afternoon I'd spent pouring over a lurid color catalog of chicken breeds. Cindy calls like it was any other day, which to Cindy it is, many moons and springs in to her chick-ordering duties, mornings that begin no doubt with the quiet sorting out of the inevitable one or two that have died in transit, to leave short wide cardboard boxes full of sprightly, dewy, loudly peeping life. I would feel very existential about that, but I'm not sure about Cindy. The practicality of a feed-store employee is a powerful salve.

*Not* feeling this was like any other day, not at all, I prepared for this morning earlier in the week, have supplies standing by, my own cardboard boxes cut and re-duct-taped together into chicken-expert recommended heights and widths. The temperature of the cannibalism-curtailing red light has been calibrated, in hourly dashes from the television during commercials to lower or raise the hanging lamp in degrees of inches, shedding enough heat but not too much to the thermometer lying in the sawdust below. This dash, from den to chick-raising pen, is possible within one commercial because, after all, the whole shebang was set up in my laundry room. I'd already raised a goat there; why draw the line now? Arbitrarily below goats and above chickens? No.

I soon discover that having the chicks in my house is an excellent idea. (Anyone who has done this knows that sentence contains foreshadowing and irony. Two months later, as I vacuumed fruitlessly into the seams and corners of shelves full of the detritus of chick life, I would discover what a bad idea it may have been. Did not learn quickly enough from the goats.) Every morning as I drink my tea, I crouch next to the box and watch this short and tiny world, discovering that the low regular peeping of content chicks is nearly hypnotizing. Which is just as well, because in my hypnotized state I have to wet my fingers and clean their tiny butts every few hours if they have anything stuck there; to not do this is to let them die. I hold their beaks into the tiny shallow cup of water so that they will know where it is. Cute does not equal smart.

One morning one chick has died. I am told this is a great percentage, only one dying in twelve. It feels like very bad odds to me. Checking in with other chick-raisers, though, I heard this *was* good, but then there is the sound somewhere in my head of another shoe dropping somewhere in the future.

Bill comes by to see my tiny charges, grinning at the insanity of sawdust and chicken feathers flying around the back room. A few neighbor girls bring their kids by during the day, holding the shooting-out hands of the children still and away from the box as fast as they could let go of one hand to grab the other. This is all certainly worth it. I have my own petting zoo, really.

I return one extremely bossy and argumentative chick to the store, which from the look on Cindy's face had to be a first in the history of chickens, since they cost two dollars. But in my house, figuring out a way to "dispose of" a troublemaker other than bringing him back whence he came was not an option. The remaining, living chicks start to get pretty big pretty fast. The edge of the box becomes a perch and the inside of my warm kitchen begins apparently to beckon, notwithstanding the snarling scramble of dogs the chicks would have to dodge to get in there.

In defense of my dachshund Honey, hunting is what dachs-hunds do best. They may lie nicely on your lap for years, but this breed was bred to hunt, judged by the AKC as the toughest dog per pound, ever. It is perhaps inevitable, though perhaps nudged along by human error, that she take a chance when finally given one to dash into the laundry room coop Christopher had built and kill as many chickens as she can reach in three seconds before I run, streaming water from the shower, slipping and falling into the coop myself, to drag some still wiggling life out of the center of the storm. For a person aspiring to raise animals, trying to come to easy terms with the cycle of the lives of small and dependent creatures, as a way to connect with nature and mortality and the world in one of the few ways deeply possible, it is a bad day.

My dachshund, who previously had not broken the soft skin of mice she'd fetched for me, has punctured the necks and breast of these three chickens in one heartbeat apiece. I pick them up and they are like rag dolls, warm and respon-sive in their flexibility. For a moment, I can't be certain they are dead. I gently try to revive two of the three, nudging their heads, curling my hand to press their wings onto their bodies, unwilling to believe it could happen so quickly. But it can.

I set each one of the three that has been killed heavily down in a box, unhappy to finally have the chance I'd wanted to see them in detail, up close, without their skittering away so fast. I have in my head a nearly wordless moment — hushed, I feel — mourning for them, very far from any sense of irony or of story or meaning: green legs, I think as I place the Americauna pullet in the box. Gray pinfeathers, I think as I set down one Welsummer pullet.

A word of advice. Don't hurry the moment, even after you are certain what you are holding is dead. Giving anything up for dead, when it is still warm, putting it in a box too fast, tidying up, is a mistake. Not for the dead, but for the living.

Chickens are often considered funny. Dumb, no personality. Mind you, this is arguably more clear if you are standing around chatting at a farm supply and feed store rather than an organic health food co-op, and I've been on both sides now, and so I waver. But among many people who raise chickens, chickens are often considered disposable: I've heard of farmers ordering enough each spring so that they will "come out ahead" after they've thrown the new chicks in with the mature ones to fend for themselves, after the predation, temperature fluctuations, and scrambling for food against bigger competition.

But if I sound harsh between the lines in my judgment of that technique, I should disclose I am not only coming to terms with a perceived failure of responsibility. To be honest, I have an unease with the finality of death, any death. Anything that dies brings me heart-fluttering anxiety, and sometimes, late at night, the memory of it brings full-blown panic. No kind of specie-ism or logic or faith divides me from it.

When I hold the small warm body of a newly dead chicken in my hand, I am not thinking of profit dollar loss. I am not immediately thinking about clamping down on the chaos of thrilled dogs, of disposability options, or cleanliness. I am feeling the thin separation of two worlds, the glimmering surface, the murky depth. I am feeling a sort of anguish, carefully but barely held in proportion to the size of the death.

Certainly, watching the surviving chickens, it is extremely clear they do not miss their fallen comrades. They only circle aimlessly, no more or less sensitive to the scene of the crime. Since chickens also kill and cannibalize each other, this comes as no surprise.

I can see myself as if from above, the day I ran outside to put a dead cat into a box (wrapped gently in one of my favorite towels; the gestures we make, the hedges we try to hold against vast meaninglessness come down to a favorite faded towel) in order to prevent the child of my neighbor, whose cat it was, from seeing it dead. The mother and I looked at each other on the road like alien species, me holding a shoebox full of cat, with tears and snot streaming down my face, her dry-eyed holding the hand of her boy, dry-eyed, whom she'd been leading to the dead body on the road without preamble. I think I'd interrupted that lesson, in death and dying, which would have helped me as a child, and supplanted it with a new one. A cautionary one: don't be like this crying woman. Thin skin is for sissies pretending the world is fair, that the world simply is not what it is. Get a grip.

But as an adult, I have to search for my lesson. Some days, it seems the less I care for death, the less quarter I give it even in my mind, the hardier I'll be in my own survival, not fraught with anxiety for the loose ends of so many lives, not distracted by the grasping, piecemeal pattern of memory, by loss of the immediate moment as it flies by untended. But I try to nail down everything with words, photographs, to-do lists, an exhausting saturation of sensory attention, all the better to hedge against the loss of consciousness that lies ahead.

On better days, I sense the lesson in the tension between caring so deeply and moving on, sense it as a nearly physical sensation of being two places at once, know it to be holding one heart in each hand. But I have now had many occasions to try to leapfrog the spiritual exercise and seek the instruction manual: Where is the book about how an animal you've cared for, lying as its heart stops in the hollow of your hand, should instruct you in dealing with the knowledge that the glorious world will survive without you in it for hundreds of thousands of years, that your heart too will stop, hopefully with the hand of one who loves you cupped above it?

That those dying near me might be at peace with their own death, or in the larger plan of nature resolved, means nothing to me on bad days. I take it all through the lens of my fear.

I'm not worried about the potential pain of a death. It's the world I want. I can't imagine ever being done with it: layer upon layer of detail and detritus waiting to be noticed and dug at, sniffed at, deciphered, embraced. With time still left, I want more time. And all this in balance with — what? What does heaven offer us that we can understand in the context of our now?

Can God just leave me with my tireless curiosity, owls at night, baby elbow crooks, the fertile smell of water, flat bright fields of snow?

Can I just have life, over and over again? Cairn after cairn of moments as moments become days, as days click together like stones?

. . .

Honey reveals the fullness of her glorious dog nature to me that day, panting at the scene, still focused, still triumphant, through the windowed glass door to the kitchen. I'd had her for many years in California and the boldest thing she'd been given a chance to do was walk too deeply into the ocean chasing seagulls, pushing her chest, no wider than my hand, against the waves. I'm not mad at her now about the chickens; I am painfully, breathlessly impressed. I had not trained her *not* to do what she's done, so she did what she knew how to do. The fault is mine.

We bring the rest of the pullets to the barn, where we finally make one of the stalls into a coop.

Going out through the cool morning or red twilight to feed those chickens, having them busing around my ankles as the feed rattled in a sandy fall into the metal trays, reaching my fingers gently deep into their warm feathers to lift them up out of corners as I looked for eggs, is all a pleasure. Driving home to see the chickens dashing recklessly around the whole yard as the cat lies resigned among them, is a good thing to come home to.

The chickens require such care, a consistent attention, the locking up of each night, the steady movement of cornering them to tend to them, the knowing they will not do a smart thing on their own ever and so you must. It suits me that they are ubiquitously mundane, nearly the joke that pigeons are to city-dwellers, and yet when the light catches their intricate feathers just so, they are ridiculously glorious, shiny blue blacks and rust reds and fleshy blush buff tans. I even like, for a while, that the two roosters we have accidentally got, a frizzle with feathers that curl twirlingly forward that I have named Blowdry, and a silky I've named Cotton, stand boldly below my kitchen window and make a stunning amount of noise. How proud they are.

Even so, I can't keep them. I have neighbors. Neighbors from whom I may need other favors and who, until now, have liked me pretty well.

So the roosters precipitate my entrance as a competitor into the Cache County Fair. I had intended to give them away at the yearly kid's rodeo in Wellsville, a free-for-all kiddie bacchanalia moment mid-rodeo when animals are set in the middle of the arena and whoever catches one takes it home. I'd attended before and knew it happened; yet when I watched one summer knowing by next fall I might donate an animal — well, it all looked a little too frantic. A twenty-second video I've got on my phone shows a boy rushing headlong to the chain-link fence right in front of me (the waving arms of children behind him makes it look like they are running from fire), and then his face thrust against the links as he dives for a rabbit, which his parents will probably make him get rid of anyway. I'd seen for myself a dad pushing a chicken *back* through the fence to be recaught once his kid had carried it proudly to the truck. I wanted better for Cotton and Blowdry.

Mandilyn and I drive down to the fairgrounds that August, me hot and pregnant and knowing I will *not* be doing this next year, not having more babies or more chickens, her unflappable with her wiggling son strapped in a car seat behind us and two sliding and squawking dog crates in the back of her 1970s mint green pickup, straw and feathers flying. She just seems to know what to do; I know her as a chic hairdresser from Salt Lake City, but she has in her a sense memory of every animal she has ever raised, fed, or shown in 4H, throughout her childhood on a potato farm in Idaho. She's just from this sort of thing. Her grandfather, a well-respected patriarch who had passed away that spring in his small town of Lynn in the extremely remote far northwest corner of Utah ("look down off the highway," she'd say to me later, "and you'll see his farm" and I see the entire cultivated floor of a valley), would have been very disappointed, I suspect, if she'd been fazed by anything so doable as juggling a two-year-old kid on one hip and a full crate of chickens on the other.

We enter the barn where the chickens will be for four days, rows and rows of cages stacked two high on top of the kind of fold-up tables used in church basements all over the world. First we fill out paperwork with a harassed lady behind a table covered in boxes and papers and stray chicken down feathers. When she says "Exotic, young?" I know she must not be talking about me, so I say, "Um, yes," with a sidelong look at my goofy breeds of prelaying, nonmature chickens. Then we must hand our chickens over to the high-school-age boy (her son) in charge of stuffing them gently into the cages. He reaches under our own hands as we delicately hold our young birds around the body with their wings protectively to their sides, and he grabs them by the legs, swinging them unceremoniously upside down, their wings flapping broadly like birds of prey and then subsiding. He walks away, I think I see, with two in each hand, bouquets of chicken feet and feathers. We can only shrug at this, and then we walk the barn to see the competition.

A man at the end of one row is methodically laying the feathers of his birds flat, gently pressing open their clawed feet to pick at any errant embedded straw. He sees us watching. "What all do you do to get them ready?" Mandilyn asks, not looking at me; he has no idea we've just turned in our own dusty straw-gripping chickens. "Oh, I do all this sort of thing, and before I get here, I bathe them," he tells us. He then tilts a bird into his hand, turning her gently on her back, to (re) clean the feathers on her belly. We walk away and Mandilyn says, "Have you ever? A bath." I admit I probably have never even seen the underside of my chickens before.

We find our own birds in their new spots, and they look pretty good on display. I'm proud to see my tag in someone else's handwriting (just like the other tags; it doesn't say "neophyte," or "new to town" or anything to give me away), "Liz Stephens, Wellsville," on the cages of my fancy well-fed birds. Under that tag I put another: "Free to good home."

Mandilyn calls me two days later. "Are you going to the fair?" Not today, I say. "Do you want to know?" she says. What? I wonder slowly, and then it dawns on me. "Did I win something?"

"We both won first prize in all our chickens' categories." This apparently is what sentimental indulgence, lavish overspending on fancy feeds, and irrepressible selection of the craziest-looking breeds, if not actual farm animal knowledge, can do. I sense it is something distantly akin to buying a great racehorse instead of training one.

My phone begins to ring an hour later. At the end of the fair, I meet a couple of strangers in the aisles of the barn, take my blue ribbons off the cages, and hand over my roosters into the new owners' little dog crates. One of the people admits she'll enter Blowdry the next year and just hope he wins again. The man that takes Cotton raises silkies; he says his neighbors hate him, but hey, they moved to the country and in the country there are roosters.

Even so, after the purge: somewhere further down the line, one more rooster reveals itself among the brood. Contrary to popular opinion, even hens sometimes have combs, and so he was able for a time to coast below the radar. However, when they'd begun laying and had all reached what I hesitantly, due to their chicken nature, call maturity, his twice daily alerts were wearing thin. I did always know when 6 a.m. and 3 p.m. were, but after all I had a clock for that. We devise a plan to drop him off under cover of night at a neighbor of Mandilyn's that she swears keeps every chicken that turns up on their place anyway, so what would they care? Clearly, we are desperate. We have not (yet?) developed the backbone we were aiming for when we chose our country home, that would enable us to boldly walk to the back pasture, pick up the bird, and twirl him in our hand by the neck — something my father did for summer money when he was young in Oklahoma, to hundreds and hundreds of birds, in addition to plucking the things afterward ("That's easy," he said. "First just plunge them in boiling water."). Not so us. Christopher enacts the plan after catching the mean bird one night, driving the back roads over, and then throwing him to the brush at the edge of this neighbor's field, in the dark, where Christopher swears the rooster starts running promptly in the right direction, headed straight for the distant coop.

Did this seem too easy?

The morning after the clandestine rooster drop, Mandilyn is able to answer that question for us. Walking out to feed her hens, she sees our rooster having his way with them. She is ticked but thinks this is still pretty funny, that the rooster has made his way across a road and two fields to arrive at her door even though, presumably, he does not know he is in the yard of friends of his former owners. Then the rooster rushes menacingly at, and attacks the lower half of, her two-year-old son. So she walks into the house, picks up a shotgun, walks back outside, and from fifty yards, shoots my rooster with one shot dead.

This is a true story. I know I should be sad, and indeed I shake my head and feel guilty (for the rooster's sake, not so much the neighbor's) every time I think of it, but then I picture Mandilyn, probably with painted toenails and sparkly flip-flops, very likely with her hair done and makeup already on for the day, possibly in a fashionable tank top and shorts, pointing that .20-gauge.

Her grandfather no doubt would have been proud.

I know something about the dark side of Mandilyn's life. I know that some days, she is vividly angry to be still living in the manufactured home where she does, when the summer heats up, and then she refuses to cook and sometimes she refuses to clean and she languishes out in the shade watching her toddler fill up a bucket from the hose over and over again just so that they can not go inside to the heat. She must glare at that cement foundation her husband poured for their future theoretical home so hard she could nearly crack it open. I know that she cried bitterly often when she was pregnant, knowing she was doing the right thing by saving money the way they saved it — one cell phone, no home phone, no television, one car. Because her husband, James, had been raised in a trailer he'd bought himself at fifteen years old, because his own father was too gone to do so and James would now be damned if he'd ever get near that perilous state again.

My favorite things she's ever said: "That rooster's been messing with that chicken and now she looks like her prom dress is all ratty in the back." And: "I'm only not Mormon because I'm lazy, and I like wine." And: "If there weren't a gin and tonic at home for me right now, I'd never go home."

I resist thinking of this new life in terms of its story-generating potential. I do. When a friend tells me she knows the death of some of my chickens will make its way into my writing, I fear a little for my soul. With this in mind I've read books on people's moves to "the country" and then been dismayed to read the online reviews of that same book, where longtime residents of these towns write, for instance, "So-and-So would like us to think she has struck out on her own in the Deep West, and furthermore makes the habits of the locals look insultingly cute."

I do not think the locals are cute and a charming part of the scenery. I think they carry within them something magic, as do, it turns out, people everywhere who have stayed still in one place long enough to accrue this grace: a deep sense of place that I wish I could beg, barter, or steal off of them.

And I am not alone in a trailer on a lonesome desert surrounded only by sage and coyotes — but if where I am doesn't represent the real and present condition of the West, then I don't know what does. Wellsville is a fairly insular and proud community. And yet I live only eight miles from the considerably larger town of Logan. I am surrounded on at least three sides by other small communities about eight miles away. And everything gets closer every day. Granted, it's forty-five miles to the closest major chain coffee place (you know the one), and perhaps that far to the closest major chain movie rental place (you know it too). If I want something as silly as Arborio risotto rice or department store face cream, I have to order it in the mail or commit to half a day of travel, there and back. But to get there, I drive by a new ocean of broken ground, where a hundred tan houses will later look like Monopoly homes jammed onto Indiana Ave. The outline of the plot of twenty acres of farmland they newly cover will be apparent by the absence of houses in the fields surrounding them, but perhaps not for long.

I guess it's clear I have feelings about this. But I don't even pretend to have the answers. Things change. Some places are just darn good places to live, and people do find out about that. Economy even needs change, I'm told. So I may not be around to see the outcome here in Wellsville. Maybe I'll sit still when I've raised a family in one place, or maybe when I'm simply too old to want to leave my familiar comforts and an easily navigated one-story home. Maybe when Christopher finally refuses to move all my books even one more time.

But for now, if things keep changing here — and even as I learn to love the place and its past, it is changing below my very feet as I go — then I believe I may have a lot farther to go than Wellsville. My answer, the one for me personally, is somewhere way out at the end of a road where any headlights are greeted with surprise. The kind of driveway the mail carrier refuses to go all the way down. The kind of place, I'm afraid, as it may be hard to find, where my memories are nonrevocable and will not be paved over.

# HEAVY IS THE CROWN

.................

can't say I was at peace the day I got the sonogram. For
one thing, I'd just had an amniocentesis, a procedure that
made even Christopher's hand twitch violently in mine as
he watched for both of us.

The specialist who performs the sonogram, and his nurse,
come in from Salt Lake City only once a month. Presumably
they are very busy, but when they begin to touch me without
introducing themselves or explaining the highly invasive procedure, Christopher steps in with his hackles up, the aggressive niceness that I know to be his most volatile state clear to
me in his outstretched hand. "I'm Christopher," he insists at
the doctor. "And this is Liz here."

Still, the doctor and the nurse are very casual with their
priceless information: "healthy," "feet," "fingers," "head," "girl."
I begin to breathe too fast. Christopher hands me up to a sitting position and I cry. I am terrified. The nurse and doctor
may think this means I will be a bad mother, as I've just clearly
by crying at exactly the wrong moment proven myself to be a
bad person, but I know this is not the problem at all.

I've just been given a kind of mandate, it feels like. Handed
a very heavy crown or mantle or stone or star or sun or animal. I'm going to raise a girl.

# THE NIGHT LIFE AROUND HERE

...............

I wake up, I imagine, to a gunshot. Gunshots are not really rare here, booming back off the mountain and from the fields nearby, and in fact, are not even as rare as they should be: one truck shoots into the holler across from us every time it passes, even though hunting from a moving vehicle is illegal, and I know for a fact that the neighbor kids used to fish down there when they were younger, and so I wonder. Still, it seems so far at least the pheasants outwit that guy every time, rushing out into the dirt road after the truck has driven on, and laughing.

But to hear that report in the dark is all wrong, the echoing impression of anger or insanity ringing with it, someone not aiming, not caring, or making a dreadful mistake. Christopher and I look at each other in bed, our ears tuned outside, where all we hear is the creek rushing into the reservoir. The noise does not sound right, reviewing it. Maybe it is our newfound fear of everything unexpected, the almost tactile sense of mortality that accompanies us everywhere since discovering we're going to be parents.

I lay back down but I know when Christopher gets up to peer toward the highway on the east edge of town, instinctively looking toward the only light we can see from our bedroom late at night, that I am right to worry. He, like me, would do anything to stay in bed right now. But he pulls on his jeans. "I'll be back," he says.

I have no premonition or intuition to guide my fear while I wait. I know that I do not like my own husband going toward possible danger before even sirens are heard, before the tidying and civilizing presence of anyone else is there to mitigate his potential hero instinct. But I do not feel less worried when I hear the sound of sirens on the highway, a few minutes after he's left.

"I'd rather not tell you," he says when he returns. "If I just tell you no kids are hurt, is that enough?" "Yes," I say, but then I say, "Tell me."

Two horses, a dam and her foal, lay dead on the highway. He tells me they were dead when he arrived, and I choose to believe him. I picture the hugeness of a horse when it lies down, picture the undeniably natural creature of which one writer said "scratch the surface of a horse and you will see how shallow its civilizing is," and I see *that* lying on the man-made surface of the road under an unnaturally bright light: an unlatched gate, a broken fence, a run in the cool sweet evening straight toward light.

A different car hit each one, cars of sober speed-limit-driving teenagers coming back into the valley, squealing to a stop as quick as they could, which is not as fast as horses pick up speed, coming at a ninety-degree angle, their pale hides rushing through the dark field.

The next morning, the gals that Christopher chats with at the gas station say it was the man right across the way. He heard the click of the gate, he said, and started running. The dam was a brood mare, he said, whose fees were building his house, sending his kids to college, et cetera. I know he cared about the horses too, but he's got his life to think about now. He said he could hear in retrospect, thinking back to nightfall, the wrong sound of the earlier click of the gate not quite shutting.

I see the pale white-yellow of the mother in the dark.

# THE WINDOWS OF WELLSVILLE

................

Charles and Johanna Bailey, Wellsville, Utah, 1900 to 1914, reads the top of a photocopy of a printout of a web page reproduction of a photograph handed to me by my back neighbor. Under the pixilated photo I read, "Johanna in front of her home in Wellsville where she moved in 1900." It is a picture of my house.

I've also been given a printout of a photograph of Charles Bailey and his nineteen sons. Other than a passing glance at his sons' resemblance to various men in town, I am much more interested in Johanna standing in front of my house. She was, I am told, Charles's second wife, and this I understand to mean not the wife he had after widowhood or divorce but the second one he married directly after the first. I don't know how many wives it took to make nineteen sons, but I know now from living here it might be fewer than you'd think. The back porch has been changed, but all the openings on the front section of the house are the same as in the photo: our bedroom window, the living room windows, our front door. Interestingly, the city's title to our house says the home was built in 1906. But here Johanna stands (because I choose to believe her, arms akimbo, fists on her hips, chin up), proving them wrong.

Aggravated that I can't see her face through the technological haze, I try to find the photo again online, to go at least one or two generations of photo back, entering first the web address as it stands at the bottom of the page, and then every permutation of it I can muster. No use; a better photo of Johanna is lost somewhere in the ether, so deeply it can't be called up. I look up "Bailey" in the phone book, since I can't think of any mailboxes bearing this name on my admittedly not-methodical drives through Wellsville, and have seen no Bailey family floats in the Founders' Day parade. There are exactly one dozen in Wellsville, with another two dozen nearby. How many might be of the sons of Johanna?

*Windows of Wellsville*, a five-hundred-plus-page doorstop of a book compiled by three women of the Wellsville Relief Society in 1984, tells me that Johanna was eventually the mother of nine children. Furthermore, I learn that her husband, Charles R. Bailey, married both her and Susannah Hawkins on "7 November 1863 . . . both splendid women and always very good friends." Johanna was from Stockholm, Sweden (a city I lived in briefly, so clean and organized it must make even city officials of Salt Lake shiver with jealousy), and she no doubt could never have imagined that not so many years after her immigration, she would "live down in the 'bottoms' in a tent to hide" from government officials hunting down polygamists, to "keep her children protected." Susannah had it no easier; her first and second daughters were two of the earliest to be laid to rest in the Wellsville Cemetery, at fifteen days and nine months, respectively. One of Johanna and Charles's sons, William (who was probably born in the room where I write this now), fathered twelve children; "all died at an early age."

Morbidly aware of my belly blooming into my peripheral vision, I can't seem to stop myself from reading this litany of mother pain. But in truth I am less caught up in the genealogy of this family, the nature of their personal workings, than

I am in the physical relevance to me: the house. I can put my hands on the house, I look through the same windows they did, I pass through the same door, out into the world and then back into the shelter of the same walls. My infant child will draw labored breath in the dormered attic room where nine other ghost babies have done the same; surely at least for the first one, and maybe for all nine, Johanna felt the same gripping fear I will when listening to the pause and resumption of a tiny chest fitfully stopping and falling and lifting again, as a new baby learns to breathe.

I am in school, urgently now trying to swallow the information in books whole, to write papers and thesis proposals, to make all my ducks line up before my deadline-making baby is born. A lot of things I'm supposed to be concentrating on are beginning to be hazy. But not this. Not the fact that my kitchen wall is two feet thick, modern plaster over the clapboard wall Joanne's husband built for her.

There's reading history and then there's this.

There's the hastily scrawled and weathered penciled phone numbers next to the dangling wires on the dingy wall of our old milking shed out back, in the room farthest from the outhouse: names I know as neighbors, numbers that may still reach the son of, or the grandson of. I know that when that buckling wall is torn down, which I guess no doubt it should be, it will take my husband holding me back to prevent me from ripping that piece of wood from the wrecking crew, because once it's gone, it's gone, that man's system of "filing," casual proof of his reliance on his neighbors and the constant movement of a small family working barn, replaced likely as not by a house of which no one may know it's past, on the site of a man's milk shed, on the site of another man's outhouse, on the land of a people who called it sacred till only one hundred and ten years ago.

# NOTCHES

...............

I do not know what any of my childhood homes look like. There is no penciled or pen-knifed notch on a wall anywhere to remind me how tall I was when. There is no little swale of earth to which I ran, in which I dreamt when I was small, that informs me and serves me as a touchstone now that I'm older. And I must admit, until recently, that simply made me feel free. Cut roughly free of my own predictably tangled and yet ploddingly mundane lot. For myself, the work of my adulthood is in building my adulthood.

And yet I have seen how these memories can deepen a life, if one has the desire to linger there. I am beginning to understand the way in which memories hold us, mindfully, to the earth, by the quality of attention paid that they require to be made at all.

Christopher's face as he recounts riding his bicycle off a specific perfect rise in his backyard into the Erie Canal, over and over, every summer till, I'm sorry to say, *college*, tells me this. "Oh, I will certainly die here," said by a woman old enough to be approaching this truth, said calmly, fondly, lovingly, tells me this.

Because for myself I begin here and now — throwing my momentum forward, even if through the pasts of others, harboring the wish that I could bank upon the memories of times

I will not ever see, seasons I won't have — because of my compulsion to gather moments to me, I want a huge span of time, in watching a place and a time change and measuring myself against it. Leaving a barn be, the work of hands long dead, hands someone loved, from the labored sawing of the tree until the boards fall out of square and in on themselves in peace, indicates the kind of span of time I'm talking about. Time to get to know a place, to note what it has been before you rush to make it what you, full of disinformation and personal baggage and the haze and hurry of your brief and present life, thought you wanted it to be.

# 4

# THE MEMORY CAIRNS

. . . . . . . . . . . . . . . . .

# HONEY

................

oney has been staggering around the house. Getting down the back stoop stairs to pee? Forget about it. In my third trimester, I lean over to pick up the small dog, pushing off the floor with my hand to lift us upright, carrying her hitched over my belly to set her in a wind-swept spot clear of snow under the pines across the yard. To get back into the warm house we do this in reverse, her damp backside pressed against me, me fighting for balance on ice as she holds her head happily, but blindly now, into the cold and fragrant wind.

She is nearly blind. She is only eleven years old, and her sister dog is completely fine. But Honey has a thyroid problem. Thyroid medicine is cheap, I've been giving it to her, but it is too little too late. Somehow I always knew she would go first; full of energy and attitude, my favorite child, I had just enough sense of the too even-handed, unfocused grace of the universe to suspect I'd lose her first. Too many lessons could be learned from losing her. I would look at her on the beach rushing optimistically at gulls and know that I loved her too much.

We call the vet for a house call, the one who came to give our horse shots and to put sweet Gus down. In retrospect that day with Gus looks easy: a dog that has had its full share of years and then some, who could no longer even stand. There was no question.

Honey is nothing but questions. Is she happy in there, inside her now well-mannered head? The vet told me on a previous visit that her new personality is due to the pressure in her brain from advanced thyroid issues, or perhaps from an additional problem, an invisible tumor. But this new attitude is *joy*. Her younger games of snarling at the other dogs, snapping at the chickens and goats, are gone, replaced with a serene expression. She leans on my hand with her full weight whenever I touch her. She turns her head to hold her nose just above my skin, smelling the person who has always been there.

But now she is stumbling into walls. She is struggling.

Christopher holds her. When the vet arrives, he hands me her collar.

After the doctor has put her down, Christopher says he and the vet sit quietly with the dog. And then he walks the man to his car, and then comes back to bury Honey.

I make him tell me everything, over and over. Once, he gives one sharp ragged sob. "I worried, just then, if I was holding Dolly. If I had held up the wrong dog." But he didn't. We will have Dolly to hold.

The hole he'd made for Gus, not long before, next to this one, was so much bigger. But I think this hole holds more. It holds the bravery and finality of my choice to be responsible. It holds my move across a country. It holds my tiny Hollywood apartment. It holds the alone time I love so much, days on the couch without anyone else but Honey, Dolly, and me. Hours and hours of driving, learning my freedom as a grownup, to see the world: the smells and excitement of gas stations and salt flats and canyon walks from Los Angeles to Vegas, of Utah fields and streams. The whole ocean. The whole desert. It holds the very first animal I chose on my own, and the first family I made on purpose.

# THE LOCAL

...............

The nurses look at me like I have a third eye as I barrage them with questions about my twenty-four-hour-old baby, before they send us home with her as if we know what to do. It finally occurs to me why they are looking at me like this. I say, "I come from a family without a lot of children." The translation for this is: I'm not Mormon. "I haven't been around babies a lot," I continue. The translation: I'm not from here.

As if the tattoos on my husband haven't given us away. As if my "advanced maternal" age hasn't meant that I've been viewed for months now by young girls in this valley as a walking apparition, something they'd seen as infrequently as I had newborn infants: a pregnant woman with a few gray hairs on her head, a little time on her face.

Certainly, the neighbors in Wellsville must have thought we were unable to conceive, now that I think about it. Christopher is prematurely gray-haired (though as he jokes, it's getting less and less premature). I'm relatively well-preserved (or perhaps only immature), but I will quickly concede that I don't look twenty-two, the apparent going age around here for first-timers. Furthermore, when we moved here, people could see by the rings that we were married, and none of them knew those rings were a scant three weeks old. It's clear, I think, from the manner Christopher and I have together that we are old friends, familiar with our own shtick, the routines that make us laugh, with the stories we tell; we've been together for years. What have we been doing, these people must think, with all that time?

In Los Angeles, our friends have, like us, just begun getting married and having children; doing either of these sooner than thirty-five makes one's friends rush in, intervention-style, to confirm that you have thought things through. For that matter, our lesbian friends have beat science to have kids before we got around to it the old-fashioned way. Thankfully, my doctor here says I'm only high-risk on the books; in person, I'm a baby-making machine. I'm thirty-eight. And I've just had my baby, here in the fruitful land of providence, surrounded by constant cycles of births, graceful Venn diagrams of overlapping circles. And she's perfect, not like a science experiment at all.

I knew I was two weeks more pregnant than anyone else thought. Including the doctor. There's a kind of math we do, at the beginning, which indicates I am this-and-such pregnant, if we count from the end of my last period, or this-and-such if you count from the day I knew I was pregnant, before that last weak hurrah of a lame period. Probably you already can tell you don't need any more details than that.

But I will say, the day I knew I was pregnant I was standing in a bathroom stall, doing the math, about to go in and teach on an unseasonably hot late May day. I knew it. I knew I'd go buy a little supermarket test, because I couldn't wait to pee on that stick, but I already knew. It was like a chemical thing, a huge rush of big good feeling, a blur of adrenaline and estrogen. I sat right on the floor and put my forehead on the cool tile, grinning.

And then suddenly it is two weeks before my supposed due date and I am having contractions and I am not surprised, sitting in the pickup truck outside a theater into which Christopher is supposed to go perform in an hour. None of either of our families is in town, wouldn't even have been on the due date, because I have already decided it's going to be just us, me and him and her. I am on the phone to the hospital with a man who is not my doctor. My doctor is out of town. "What would you have me do, if I were your patient?" I ask.

"Well, I'd say get on in here and let's feed you some Pitocin and get you going and have that baby."

"And when is your shift over?" I ask.

Christopher does not perform that night. The author of the play, given forty-five minutes' notice, bravely shaves his head (the character is an army sergeant) and walks on stage and bellows those lines like a pro, just the way he wrote them.

I hold out until 7:00 a.m. when Mr. Hail Fellow Well Met's shift is over.

It is a long birth. I eventually go for all the drugs. The man who gives me my epidural pauses when he lifts my gown and sees the big tattoo of wings on my back, wings that aren't taking me anywhere, just when I need them to. He covers his surprise by telling a story about a woman who drove herself in from harvesting to have her fifth or sixth kid, "just stepping out of her overalls," and I feel connected to that tradition even in my wimpy take-me-to-Jesus state.

We use every tool in the book, everything I worried about for months, and none of that matters. I just watch the top of the sweet head appear in the mirror. This doctor is lovely. He eventually quietly tells my husband that if I can't make it happen on the next push, they're prepping the cesarean room. Christopher thinks I haven't heard the doctor, but by God

I have. The room is full of people I don't know, five nurses with an intensive care cart of machines, my primary nurse, an intern, a delivery guy who's a friend of the doctor, who leans in around the door at just the moment the baby is born to holler hello, and then is rooted to the spot by awe. I forgive him. Good Lord, I forgive everybody.

Whether my insular surrounding community sees my family or me as authentic, valid, or entitled to try, or that holiest of grails, *local*, has become slightly more distant, pushed at least to the edge of my little acres by the burgeoning amount of life fenced within. I made a decision to write about the West as I was seeing it as a newcomer. But living here, as living does, means my life is to a great degree simply becoming my life. Yes, I still feel the frisson of unexpectedness in moments, but it comes more and more slowly, less and less often — maybe when I'm standing in front of a morning class, realizing that I've already fed a dozen chickens in the dark of morning, when I'm just about still asleep, climbing two pipe fences at six months' pregnant to dig layer feed out of the bag in the tack room, nudging aside my not-intelligent charges to set the metal feeder among them, weaving through drowsy horses to trudge back to the house. As much as I want to feel I belong, as I lose my sense of outsider resonance — shedding the irony I was after all trying to outrun — I feel sometimes as if my sounding is off, my bearings indistinct.

Will bearing, *having*, my child in the West give her citizenship? In the way that immigrants struggle to the States to birth and thus bequeath to their offspring something they themselves as parents may never have: the whole weight of unequivocal membership, in a culture they themselves longed for? I may always be tinglingly aware at a barely conscious level of the theatricality of my consciously chosen life, the sensation of watching myself over my shoulder — but she won't. That is, sometime until around the age of ten, when a kid from another place says, "You grew up riding horses in the mountains? You had chickens?" She may suddenly have a sense of the coinage of her life, the mileage she can get out of telling people where she's from. It may dawn on her that what she could know as normal life is considered by others as anachronistic, rare, special, interesting. But it appeals to me more to not trade on this, to keep her in places where anachronistic has no meaning while I can. To let belonging to somewhere be built into her, wherever else she goes. Of course she'll move away from me, and likely from here, because she is my daughter, because she is a daughter in the twenty-first century. But we can be her fall-back plan, and her stash of memories. Her deep and wide past.

Emerson writes that "no one expects the days to be gods." But now, as time flies and a baby will grow in a place of my choosing, I know. The days are gods. They are each unrepeatable and each a lesson in scope and wholeness, each worth honoring. I can hold and turn these days, consider their resonance, dim and bright moments, sound the depth and know the lullingly measured length. And know that for the time being my memories, and the days in which they are created, are not the only ones of which I'm in stewardship.

# FINDING OKLAHOMA

. . . . . . . . . . . . . . . . .

I myself was raised in the Midwest. My memories are not far outside my body, and thus are usually loose from context: Buzz of cicadas. Sweating at night. How ticks could be anywhere. Hills of trees. The lake where hippie college students sunbathed nude. Running down ditches when it rained, snapped fast into my swimsuit, in the bit of time between the drizzle and the thunder.

My parents were both from Oklahoma. It took many years for it to sink in to me that they too, as I was destined to, had left the place where they'd grown up, all of us racing from our pasts, just because we could.

Both sides of my family are a common American blend of what were likely eighteenth-century English businessmen, nineteenth-century Irish field workers, a couple of French fur traders, and a few Native American tribes, mostly the Cherokee and the Choctaw, both of which were forced west into, and then out of, Oklahoma on the Trail of Tears. None of this mattered to my folks when they were little, of course, when the appearance of a full-blood Indian was as surprising as a black man in town. My mother remembers having a pony named Patches in the corner lot beside their house and her sisters putting their dress slips into the freezer so they could slide them on cold. My father remembers leaping onto the back of the ice truck as it went down his street to nick ice chips with the delivery man's blessing, and the woman next door taking eggs from his family's backyard coop one day when she thought they were all at church.

My mother was a town girl, such as it was — I imagine *Last Picture Show* — but my dad was still a little closer to a farming background. Or maybe, now that I think about it, it was the difference between being a girl and a boy, because my father's father was certainly a white-collar man. But my dad walked out of town every day one summer to run the farm of a friend who'd broken a leg; he also raised chickens for extra money as a teenager. (When I got my chickens, he said, "Well, I wouldn't wish that on anyone.")

I'm not mentioning this all by way of tracing my own country and small-town desires lineally, though as I see the list of all they'd done it begins to seem that way, surprisingly resonant. Really, all these stories seem like fantasy to me, so far are they from the college-educated and -oriented people I know, the Arts and Crafts furniture collectors, the northern city transplants. What I'm wondering, sitting here on my tiny precarious ledge of contested entitlement, is what would it take, when you move to the West, to not be viewed as an upstart? You can't help but be an outsider. You can't go back and be born there. But what can you not be? Rich? Academic? Aggressive for progress? Regressive for romanticism? Urban? From California?

None of these help.

I am combing my background for traces of Americana that resemble, inform, or presage my rural Utah experience. Ridiculous, some sense that I can build a case for my membership here. But what I unearth about my family's history is a revelation to me, the story of myself before myself.

In the heat of high August in Oklahoma, I sit in my rented economy car, next to the Girl Scout camp trash bin next to a building through the windows of which I can see stacks of folded folding tables. I have taken another research trip, this one on my own dime, because how does one explain in a grant proposal that you have to go see your family? I am trying to run my understanding of myself to ground. The timing is horrible; I can't even think about the baby, who's like drugs to me, or breathing or food, something dire and necessary, or I'll have to change my shirt. The crickets are loud, the sky is oppressively bright. The cheat-oak trees have crept forward, sneaking through the years to loom heavily over the gravel lot where I sit. I am looking at my father's land.

My siblings and I have heard about it for years, this five acres my dad bought when he and my mom got married in 1953, land that now abuts the back corner of a summer camp. Some atavistic sense of a man needing to own land to be truly adult and ready to support a wife guided him, I'd guess, though he's never said that exactly. The act seems uncharacteristically romantic and frivolous of my father now, but I try to picture him at twenty, black hair and future gaze, with the longest eyelashes my mother had ever seen. Five acres when I'd first heard about it had sounded like a baron's share, room for anything we could dream up as a family for which to use it. Five acres has shrunk since then. Still, I see that the relative wildness of this spot, this charming snarl of green near Turner Falls, a place families visit every weekend as a respite from the interminable flat of so much of Oklahoma — there's an appeal to its hidden quality.

But I'm not supposed to be here anyway. My dad had told me not to bother the Girl Scouts, an annoyance in his e-mail I could almost hear. The brisk waving hand one uses at bees, a shrug. A "why bother?" A lot like the reaction of his own mother, nearly thirty years ago, when I'd asked her as a young and dreamy girl if she'd ever had chickens. (I was young. I didn't know that raising chickens in your backyard was so common and was ubiquitous two generations ago. Forgivably; this was also around the age when I thought the movie *Ben Hur* was filmed in ancient Rome.) "Of course I did," she'd said. "But that's not interesting." She loved my siblings and I dearly and made us all the peach cobbler we could eat, but she didn't think to lead me ten steps to that very backyard where she could have shown me precisely the spot where the coop had sat.

I go back to see her house too, on this trip. The whole home stands a slumping ghost on its heat-baked corner lot, and the house across the way a ghost as well, literally draped with vines. I should have known better than to dwell in this neglected neighborhood, all signs pointing to this being a bad idea, but I cup my hands around my eyes and lean onto the dusty windows of my father's childhood home. I know which room I'll see, I remember all of that, but I am amazed at its smallness. And at its ruin. Mounds of old carpet, the curling of the wood paneling. This is the room where I saw my first Christmas tree. This is the room where my sister and I wore our grandma's Eastern Star tiara and sat on her fancy vanity chair pulled from the bathroom for the purpose of sitting on while wearing the tiara. This is the room where I weighed my grandfather's silver dollar collection in my hands and was impressed. This is what happens when no one is there to dust, nail, tinker, and cook, open the windows each morning and close the shades on the full-loved rooms at dusk.

The shine of the memories I placed within those walls was bright. I'd had no idea how much I'd wanted those intact. However, like Dad's land, too small to be valuable, just large enough to be a bother, this house will be ignored. No one will ever paint it again. And I'm not mad at anybody. This is just the way things go; close up, with my own family to question, I can see that. Who has time for every old house in the world? Right?

I remember while standing there a derelict house I'd snuck into in Los Angeles, a house to which a real estate agent had directed me, which had a million-dollar view but was in a quarter-of-a-million-dollar neighborhood (cheap by L.A. standards). The house itself was considered a teardown. I'd stepped anyway into the back door, found through the tiny backyard a dim and cool time warp. I found myself surrounded by the detritus, the quiet winding down, of a woman's life, a widow who'd kept to herself for years and finally passed. Relatives, her children and their children, had presumably combed the place for all they wanted, the furniture and photos and silverware. Yet on the kitchen wall hung a tiny sketch of a dog, framed, some unbearably corny saying penciled in near its mouth. I lifted it off its hook, off of the pale piece of wallpaper revealed below it, the shape of the frame still hanging on the wall. I knew the walls were coming down any day. So I took it. I left with the framed sketch in my hand, some anonymous woman's memory, a little thing from a magazine she'd found charming enough to take the time to frame. I still treasure it, and not because it's charming on my wall (it's irredeemably tacky: "Friends are forever!"), but because it makes me think of anonymous her, living placidly in the sun, gardening with her back to the million-dollar view. The little dog has the same mysterious quality I've always attributed to the taped-up cutout household hints I often find inside the kitchen cabinets of old houses I've bought or rented, a yellow and crackly piece of newsprint, and not moved by me, never removed by me, an act that would be in my mind a kind of hubris.

Sometimes I long for practicality, the lack of sentimentality, which allows my family to forget this little white house and frees most people to just get on with things. On the other hand, there is the person in my family, who surprisingly is not me, who keeps nearly every scrap of paper she's ever touched, just in case, just in case the world is ending and everyone has enough food and water but needs ephemera, needs slips of paper, needs old articles and wrapping paper and tax documents and someone else's past to stand in for the past of us all.

I hover somewhere between these two worlds, saving some memories, letting others fritter and slip away. Down one of these paths, it seems to me, the obsessive compulsive holding on and the equally aggressive letting go, lies madness, and even I don't know which one. Culturally and personally both — who can say, which path leads to the better place?

I guess I wince when my cousin-in-law says, standing at a Choctaw powwow with me in Oklahoma City, that "the ones who are the worst are the people that say they just *feel* Indian, spiritually, and so they must be." She sees my expression and says firmly, "Oh no. You *are* Indian."

Am I?

It's a story I've told about myself for a long time, trotting out when the context arose for it, the one even slightly exotic thing about me. The factual knowledge of my smidgeon of partial blood status had long since taken on this quality of a story. To be reminded that not so very far back, full-blood Choctaw men and women held some of the seeds that would eventually lead to me is — chastising. They were not a good story, they are real. Two of my great-grandparents were likely full-blooded Choctaw, and a few of my other great-grandparents were half Cherokee or part Catawba, so I am as much as a quarter Indian, "put together."

But it seems a narrow thing, statistics, on which to hang one's identity. I am not registered with the Cherokee tribe, but I am a card-carrying Choctaw tribal member. Still, am I a Choctaw Indian? Culturally, this feels unanswerable. I so far am too wary to trade on something so heavily meaningful to others who have no choice but to identify as Native by the nature of their skin and features. My cousin, who does identify more readily as Native, tells me it takes a lot of work to remain in good standing, as a man who is mostly white. Yet I see the depth of his life, willingly entangled with history and tradition and obligation. I *want* to burn sage for its meaning rather than its smell, I want the rituals. But so far this is yet another way of life I feel I haven't earned, just as I feel about moving West into ranch country, even though this native life is literally in my blood. So I carry it privately, passing for 100 percent white and rightly so as I am *so* culturally white, knowing somewhere in me I carry deep roots, to something, to somewhere I haven't explored, but to which someday I may feel myself more entitled, or obliged, to claim.

When I ask, nearly whispering, why more people are slowly becoming part of the performance at this powwow, joining the circles of dancers and drummers in a stream, seeing a growing strength and power in the intention, in the pattern of bod-ies gathering, my cousin tells me, ever so politely: "They just found parking."

My aunt is nothing if not nonchalant. Calm, classy, always the art school gal from somewhere else for all of her sixty years here in southeastern Oklahoma. Well known to be unflappable in, for instance, cutting off a cat's tail (it was infected) or steering deliberately into oncoming traffic as she turns (protected by grace, instinct, and her boat of a Lincoln Continental), she is extremely casual as she points out, "That was Phillip's letter jacket." Phillip was my mother's brother, this aunt's late husband; he died twenty years ago. The jacket hangs on the wall of the local historical museum in Sulphur, Oklahoma. "That was the shop I owned," she murmurs, waving at a waxed paper shopping bag artfully set into a display marked "Old Sulphur." "There's Phillip," she points, in a collection of high school photos from any year the archivists could find, between nineteen-oh-something and 1980. Phillip, small and nimble, before gaining the weight of his voracious appetites, before age, before cancer, seems in motion even in this still photo, a boy in a football jersey leaning right, running fast, the ball in his arms about to go with him through the goal posts.

An amateur historian's book — and bless and keep these amateur historians, and the impulse that drives them, I think as I page through — includes the brother and wife of my grandfather on my father's side, born and married as all my relatives of that generation were in Oklahoma when it was the I.T., the Indian Territory. I comb through the historic grade school photos of the early 1940s, willing my parents' faces to leap out at me. They don't but the discovery seems so close; these photos bear an identical look to those in my mother's wicker baskets, the same bowl haircuts, same sagging socks.

Out in front, when I tell an old, old man who my people are, he says, "Oh, yes, well, everyone my age remembers Ira Stephens. He was a fine woodworker." I am almost forty, *and* my parents had me late; this man must be in his late nineties. I have almost missed him; he just happens to be standing here, at lunchtime, in summer, in the melting heat, making me want to hold my clutch of brochures over his dear head for shade.

And it is the first time I have heard anyone from outside my family remember anyone in my family ever, in this past and communal way, memories that belong to them but not to me. But here they all were, the memories and the rememberers, the whole time. I am the one who is gone.

Each of my cousins owns and runs cattle on more than three hundred acres apiece. Many lives, many layers of time, have revealed themselves on these seas of land that were once a vast ocean: the sedimentary stone traced with the shapes of sea-water-origin skeletons, the disrupted grasses that reveal the footprint of settlers' homes, the anonymous bones of other people's cattle from before the land was fenced at all. On one of these seas stands a graveyard, subsumed in the property of one of my cousins, a tick-filled, barbed-wire-fence-laced maze.

I stand in the unlikely shade alone, shielded from the August sun everywhere outside this tiny square by the surprisingly dense understory of the trees that crowd the graves. I am in love with cemeteries, surprising given that I am not a friend of death. I walk, I nearly crawl, through the place, not wanting to miss paying my respects (or superstitious dues) to any one of the few dozen stone markers, running my hands lightly over the inscriptions, sitting back on my heels to consider the intention of each family in their choice of stones and words, pondering the year of death, the age of each interred. One stone bears the surname of the opposite side of my family; I am less surprised than I might have been in the past, before Wellsville, at the smallness of community this indicates. The only modern marble stone is crisply carved with its name, a soldier who died in 1949, and whose family went through the trouble to find this spot within the last few years, and asked for permission to place this stone; I am curious to know what they thought when they finally found this place at the end of their search. All the other graves are earlier, many from 1903, a sickness running through. There are huge patches of leaning lilies, which propagate abundantly over time and now cover whole squares of family, too systematic to be accidental, too wild and organic in their form now to be pretty, too shady to bloom but bright enough to grow their persistent green clumps of lanky shoots. I stand over this odd carpet, this insistent life, and gaze out at the sunny field beyond the wire fence. Birds sing, cicadas click their slow hot daytime standing-by click, warming up for their epic night orchestration. The horses of the surrounding field stare at me curiously, leaning toward me over the drooping wire fence with an indifferent and calming lack of respect for the dead over which they swing their heads. I watch them watching me.

The weight of a heavy mortal fear I carry lifts briefly, allowing me a tenuous moment when I can view — or at least see how others can view — death as practical, cyclical, natural; can hold the thought of death, with my breath held, slightly closer to me; the kind of moment that I hope will eventually lead me backward into healing. If this is the worst that can happen — your burial forgotten by all but time, untended by family, in a place wildly lovely in its insistent and inconvenient presence — I could live with this. Live with the knowledge, I mean, and then someday, die with it. Maybe I can even wish for this. Not a bother to anyone, but just here, somewhere, on the face of the earth.

It is not the only cemetery I see on this trip. When my aunt asks if I'd like to drive over to the Sulphur town cemetery where my extended family is buried, I am still out of synch enough to be thinking of other things — whether the Sonic is still open down the way, how quickly the car will cool off with the air on high. You'd think a person seeking history and family would have thought to actually plan a trip to the place where her relatives are buried. But the experience of seeing the burial stones of people I know is so removed from my life, it *never occurred to me.*

But there they were, the grave site of my mother's mother, a woman I'd known and loved but whose grave I'd never seen, never thought to seek, and her husband beside her, his death thirty years before her own, my mother's father whom I'd never met. This as I stood next to my aunt's car and looked at the grave of her own husband, a stone placed twenty years ago. So many women living on and living on. My aunt in true Oklahoma style never gets out of her car, and coasts beside me down the gravel lanes with the window down, sitting comfortably in the air-conditioning of the Lincoln. "Your dad's folks are here somewhere," she ventures thoughtfully. "But I'm sure I don't know where."

"What does the proverb on Phillip's say?" I ask about her husband, my uncle's, headstone.

"A cheerful heart is good medicine," she paraphrases, gesturing me back into the passenger seat. We drive a moment in silence, slowly back toward the cemetery gates. "Do you know how many people are dead and buried in this cemetery?" she asks. I don't know. "All of them," she says, and looks at me and laughs.

The sweetest laugh, not forced, no edge, no bitter gallows humor, a light sound in the harsh loud brightness of the day, lifting into the cloudless sky. It's the punch line she'd been trying to get right during that silence in the car. I certainly don't know why some hesitation keeps me from asking just then what the proverbs are, whose numbers are carved into the large family stone itself. But when I look up Proverbs 3:5 and 6 later, they are these: Trust in the Lord with all your heart, and do not rely on your own insight. In all your ways acknowledge him, and he will make straight your paths.

I had visited Oklahoma years ago as an adult but with my parents, and my primary interest that time had been the lifestyles of my cousins, this brood of men and women who collectively own and/or are now related by marriage to those who own a significant chunk of southeastern Oklahoma land. The ranches, the animals, the rodeo circuit work, the local histories traced by stories with a location, a map of moments lived: juvenile car accidents on rural roads, babies born in hospitals where parking lots now stand, children married, business deals, houses built, money lent and borrowed, here, here, and here. The stories of a family embedded in their place.

On this trip, I am taken aback to recognize that I, along with my siblings, am part of their stories: Ice cream hand-cranked beside the pool the year the pool water was hotter than bathwater, the way Aunt Berta's place used to look before the town widened the road and killed her bushes, the chicken strip lunches at Annie's Snack Hut the summer my cousins were life guards next door, the year I got a tick in my *eye* at the dead-end of my aunt's road, which of course is no dead-end now, the fact that I know which chair is my uncle's chair in the den twenty years after his death. The fact that I not only remember but attended the drive-in movie down the road from where my grandmother lived, a drive-in so thoroughly gone you can hardly even find it in our national memory, much less under the bright electric hum of the car dealership lights now haloing the spot. The sharp and specific memory of not the car dealerships and insurance offices that surround my grandmother's house now, but the small one-pump gas station I could see from her guest room at night, the exoticism of her living in the one house on the highway with that one bulb swinging in the wind across the way, its light on the pump under the awning the reason I love paintings by Edward Hopper to this day. This common history is the reason my relatives look at me as patiently as if I were doing a high school genealogy paper (which is to say, very patiently, very sweetly, possibly feeling a little bit bad for me) as they ask, over and over, "But what are you writing *about*?" They see me plodding around Oklahoma, looking for memories that I recognize, ones that bear to me a family resemblance. I'm looking for proof that I may reach into a time longer than my own blip on the radar, further into meaning something about all of us, yet in a way that selfishly extends the meaning of *me*. Putting what will be the memory of me in tandem with a larger story, a stronger tide, the better to leave a deeper — unsightly, selfish, and still ultimately temporary — mark on the land.

And remember this anyway, before I burrow in too comfortably: I am borrowing these stories too, just as I do in Wellsville, these stories in which I appeared as a tiny supporting character if at all. My immediate family left, left behind themselves their parents' homes, their brother's letter jacket, their drive-in movies, their high school smooching-lanes, their drag-strip main street, the drugstore where they got cherry Cokes and dime novels off a swiveling circular rack, the pool where they learned to swim, their parents' graves. These are stories I have pasted together and drawn out in the telling. I was not surrounded and carried forward by these stories as I grew up. No one I went to school with would have known any of this about my family, about me. I did not know this about myself.

And then I rush home to my tiny baby, where Christopher

holds her in the airport, and I rip her from his arms as if he'd made me leave in the first place. Five days to go find out about forty years.

I am more instead of less confused now about where I'm from. I am more instead of less confused about why it should matter to anyone else. Maybe I simply replace some errant western daughter, in a huge holistic circle of energies. Or perhaps we never can repair the holes we make in others' lives, and our own, by moving on.

When I get home — *home* — I slow down when I'm speaking, and also when I'm listening, realizing no one but me is in a hurry when chatting over fences, or from window to window of idling cars on the dirt road past the reservoir. I talk to my Wellsville neighbors not about my own questions on history, place, the meaning of life entire, laboriously applying my metaphysical yearning to their lovingly quotidian lives, but about what they bring to me, subject-wise: family, church, horses and hunting, canning and quilting. I latch all gates behind me carefully, as even the tiniest of kids here will do, and I don't talk badly about anyone's children to anybody ever, no matter how inexplicable their behavior. I make pies for new mothers. It all seems to help.

# OH COUNTRY ROADS

.................

I drive the back road to Mandilyn's house. Mostly the drive is all back road, because she lives on one and I live on one. The highway between us can be avoided too, by aiming for the mountain and crawling along near its bottom.

I make this drive at nearly all times of day and night. At twilight it is the most beautiful thing, bar none, that I have ever seen. The entire drive is a sequence of postcards. Mountain in fading light, idyllic isolated farm, young horses running in cool air, glimmer of creeks, falling fence posts propped with cairns of field stones, capped with cow skulls and western meadow larks.

Today, another run-of-the-mill stunning twilight, a horse stands in the road in front of me. Somewhere between the trailer with the roosters and the river with the redwing blackbirds, this horse stands silhouetted in the falling sun.

No one attends him. No one but me and the horse here alone on this back road. Pulling my truck over is pretty beside the point; throwing on the hazards even seems like overkill. I sigh at the horse. We look at each other for a while. He's dirty.

I knock on the door of the nearest house, but I'm already sure that somewhere a grown son or a grandson or granddaughter sits playing video games, not feeding their own horse. The house looks like grandparents' houses the world over. An iron birdbath that has definitely gone out of production since the Korean War tilts behind a short "novelty" fence that wouldn't really keep anything out or in. Another horse stands on a practically vertical mud hill across a wandering ranch road from the house. I eye it, because it's going to matter as well.

She shuffles slowly to the door, a door with a small index card taped to it: "I'm here," the card says. (Later, when I tell my brother, "She was as sharp as a tack, she could remember everything," he says, "Well, the little cards help.")

"Takes me a while," she says, even as she's opening the door.

"I don't mind," I say. "But your horse is out."

We both stare at the horse standing placidly in the road enjoying, seemingly, the last of the sun. She looks at my shoes.

"Yep," I say. "I'll get him."

"That other horse nips at him, makes him mad."

It's not easy to corner a horse by yourself. There is naturally more convincing than cornering. Still, I have caught all my neighbors' horses or calves or sheep at one time or another, day or midnight, in all seasons, and it has never ceased to be a joy to me, to be useful and knowledgeable at once. Correspondingly, I now have opinions about people's fences. I read local news for the laws and fines pertaining to downed fence. I watch the top line of fences as I drive, instinctively, and eyeball the turn of wire with sticks over rivers, dead man's hangs, for tautness, as I go by.

Ultimately, I get him just by laying a rope around his neck and pushing him where he knows he ought to go. He's not thrilled.

And the old lady is right. That other horse, waiting at the fence, is even meaner.

But I make it to Mandilyn's by dark.

# WEDNESDAY NIGHT LIGHTS ACROSS FROM THE STOP-N-GO

.................

I t is summer when the convenience stores are papered in curling flyers for rodeos. Local rodeos are competitions for whoever can pay the fee, which goes toward paying the guy who brought the stock (the cows for penning, the bulls for riding). If you think professional rodeo is rough, you should see the amateurs; I get a lot more scared for the guy about to jump on a bull when he himself looks worried. And even though the much louder razzing you hear in small rodeos from the waiting riders in the chutes is comforting somehow, casual, the lack of an ambulance standing by is not great. Somebody could be going to the hospital in a beat-up tiny Honda, trying not to bounce on his own broken leg, crammed and folded into the passenger seat. Or he might make the ride with his buddies bracing him against a side of the flatbed of a truck, lying down prone but in the rushing night air. We just all hope that won't happen, and sit eating the snacks we've brought from home in the stands, yammering away talking to neighbors and taking cell phone calls from more boring, less companionable places where we presently are not.

There is lots of talk about whose stock it is being ridden or roped, about which of the riders is on or was on the high school team. There is talk about who left whom in which now apparently not eternal Mormon marriage, and what day the farrier (the "shoer") is coming to your neighbor's house, and can he come by your place too. There is talk of returning missionaries and invitations to come see them speak in church. There's a lot of caffeine-free-Sprite drinking. And every once in a while, there's a ride so fine everyone shuts up and turns around, a perfect turn around every barrel a blast of horse galloping legs a full eight seconds an explosion of animal talent or human willpower that no one not there will ever see, no televised replay, no newspaper journalist with pen and a camera slung at the neck, nobody the next day when you tell them at work or in line or online. Just the few dozen people who drove over after dinner to sit on the splintery stands, gathered like a cupped hand under one streetlight on a pole that isn't shining on street. It makes a circle of the dirt and horses and calves, of the old wooden arenas that look like the WPA may have built them in 1930. And then we all go home.

I'd invited a couple of friends to come to this small weekly rodeo with Christopher and me once. I kept meeting others about our age who had left cities nearby, come to the valley to raise horses and live on a dirt road. This made me want to know them, because trying to explain why thirty wasn't really old to younger locally raised grad students was getting a little tiresome. But the phenomenon of finding the others did unsettle me, knowing always that only so many of us transplants could do this before we'd reach the tipping point and tip over and find ourselves sitting in a Barnes and Noble or Gap somewhere on overpriced ranch land thinking "What have we done?"

Our new friends yoo-hooed me over to them at the fence when they arrived late and tipsy, and I had to blink against the setting sun to be sure I was seeing them right. They were in costume, basically. They had theme-dressed for the rodeo. Hats I'd never seen on them before had been pulled from closet shelves somewhere, presumably in their own house; boots pulled from their crush under sneakers and pumps and Tevas, shaped and shined and shoved on. Lots of gingham and metal snaps were happening.

I tried not to judge. I was just barely past this myself, I reminded myself. Barely. There but for the grace of God go I. And anyway, what's more authentic? Their giggly "yee-haw" field trip to the rodeo or my brand-new self-satisfied homey feeling? Honestly?

# AVOIDING JACKSON HOLE

................

**M**y tiny daughter is being held by Camille while Camille rides her horse. Christopher can barely watch, it makes him so nauseated with anxiety. "That's an old horse," I remind him. "And, well, they're still in the round pen." I point out the obvious, though we both have seen some seriously violent surprises go down in these twelve-by-twelve-foot circles. I picture standing outside the round pen at Bill's while aggravated horses kick the metal over and over again, dogs at the edge tumbling over themselves to get away from the reverb, the unbelievable racket. I picture the day I watched as Christopher swung himself up onto my horse, and I knew before his butt hit that he'd be thrown off for his hard and fast attitude, and he was. Twice. I can see Bill running a rustling plastic bag over a horse's side, a horse he's just made lie down, all fifteen hundred pounds stretched in the dust, in order to teach it not to startle and in the meantime its legs kicking, seeking to connect with anything and enact revenge.

But there Camille rides in the sun, cooing at my girl who is small enough to hold up with one broad hand against her, plodding about on the horse with dogs running underfoot. I hold my breath until I can't anymore, and then say, "All right. I'll take her." I don't admit the sensation out loud to Christopher, the blurred image in my brain of sunny dusty walking horse and whirring hooves.

Camille also carries the baby around rodeo chutes and stock-yards. She hitches the baby on her side and takes off to chat with the rodeo boys from town, idly lifting the baby's small hands to touch flanks and stirrups, as absentmindedly as if the hands were her own, though the baby gazes mesmerized at the horsehair and plaited leather under her fingers. I sit in the shade of wooden arena stands and remember that this is how Camille herself was no doubt raised, and still there she stands, strawberry blond and sunburned, her solid and confident stance defying anyone to knock her off her feet.

On the other hand, she's only seventeen. What does she know?

But heck, what do I know? So it goes, in a big circle, but the kid lives on unharmed in my and Camille's care.

Camille won't accept payment for any Sunday hours, but insists on coming by. We pay her far too much for the weekday hours because we have no idea what the going rate is and cannot sense where the line lies between neighborly favor and teenage desire. She later buys a very fine saddle with all the money she makes that summer. A *very* fine saddle.

I take the baby camping in Yellowstone. She'll sleep anywhere, and I have the photo from the night before to prove it: her arms flung out in decadent, luxurious trust, dozing like a puppy in the dent of a blow-up mattress on the ground. Now I am sitting on the tailgate of my truck at a gas station outside Jackson, Wyoming. It is late afternoon, and I have just sworn and spit my way through a couple hundred miles of the most scenic driving in America. I have unwisely and against all recommendations taken the south exit out of Yellowstone National Park, in spite of the fact that we'd camped at the northwest corner of the park, just inside the west Montana entrance. Insistent tracing of my map with my finger indicates to me that the path back through the park and then south past the Tetons, down through Jackson, through the southeast corner of Idaho, then through Logan Canyon to home, is clearly the way to go. I am hesitant to add that the friend recommending the alternate west exit, get-out-to-Highway-15-and-head-straight-south-on-a-four-lane-highway path, actually *works* at Yellowstone. This would make me look pretty dumb, I guess.

Driving past Shoshone Lake, when I was still within the park, I was a little aggravated at the slow speed limit, but the lake itself is some dreamy combination of Narnia, what I imagine East Coast lakes to be like, and a living excerpt from Lewis and/or Clark's journals. I stopped my truck and stood at the edge among the pine trees, the roots of which twist and drop abruptly into the clear water at my feet. Due home in a few hours to make dinner for multiple guests, I was pleased at the day ahead of me. But I was not doing the math: it had taken me nearly as long to get to the south exit of the park as it would have taken to get halfway down through the corner of Idaho toward Wellsville.

By the time I am crawling below the Grand Tetons, the slabs of granite and snow rising to God viewed across golden green fields traversed by noble buffalo, I am one palm-slap away from riding my horn down into Jackson. Uncharitable thoughts, even about my beloved adopted West, cloud my thinking. "How much," I am thinking, "of this view does one actually need? Do all these drivers really need to see this mountain in slow motion for quite so many miles?" It is after all a barely changing view from the time you enter the open fields after Grand Teton National Park at the north till you are nearly into Jackson, a distance of some forty miles.

I whip through Jackson, a town I had waited to see for

years — on my first visit, we'd taken the requisite pictures of each other, Christopher and I, under the antler arches in the square, we'd sat on the saddle bar seats at the Million Dollar Cowboy Bar, we'd had our photo taken in Old West costumes and overpaid for the sepia-toned print a computer churned out for us — I'd even mushed a penny through a machine that stamped it to say "Welcome to Jackson Hole, WY."

Today, however, I will absolutely be damned if I'll be forced into stopping for gas in this tour-bus-congested mouse-maze warren of streets, full of cameras and more-hat-than-cow cowboy hats and children wearing absence-of-matter black, right-off-the-rack black "Harley-Davidson of Jackson, WY" T-shirts that will surely cover their hot backs and bellies in black lint fur by tonight at the motel, streets full of men hunched over crisply creased maps of Wyoming while their sweaty family stares mutely from inside the car at every gas pump in town. No. I will wait until I am through town, way past the trailers where the "actual" people live, until I stop to hunch over my own map. I take a deep breath of harsh, dry, wild country as I sit on the tailgate of my truck wedged next to the motorcycle tire I keep in the back, which secures the straw that I used last winter to get out of an icy mud spot in my back pasture. Everything is a bit of a mess; my truck, my plans, myself, my sticky baby. A smallish SUV pulls up next to me. The window scrolls down with an audible sigh.

"Excuse me," a woman drawls out the window. She looks at my truck, she looks at my hair, gathering a sense of me in general. What does she see? I'd be hard put to say, anymore. Their plates are from somewhere else; maybe I see a peach on one. "Do you know where the KOA is?" I do know where the Jackson KOA is. "Just north on this road," I say, "across from the saddle shop." They drive away.

I have come a long way to be sitting at this gas station. Home isn't one structure, not really; it's a fabric of things, humid versus not humid, lightning bugs or scorpions, trees or rocks, dirt roads or paved and manicured and street-lamped. Because it is the region with which I first identified, it seems like frosting to also have a tiny house on land I love, tucked under the lee of a mountain that always surprises me, where I always feel as if I'm dreaming: barn, chickens, snow, mountain, dirt road, vegetable garden, husband, baby, life, life, life. The peace I feel here on this land, and in that house, is rare to me, a silence that starts somewhere deep and comes forth to hover just under my skin. I think I know now where I will always be "from." This is not always, as one might have supposed, a past tense kind of thing.

# THE REENACTORS

.................

I t is fall when mountain men stock up for the winter. My
husband and his bachelor friend Luke stand lingering in the
middle of the dirt walking path, in Blacksmith Fork Canyon,
down Left Hand Fork, amid tepees and columns of smoke rising from cooking fires.

"You're so obvious," I tell them, the baby on my hip gazing
around wide-eyed from under the brim of her brand-new pio-
neer-style bonnet. They are trying to work up Luke's courage,
but he can't think of anything to say to the ridiculously lovely
girl doing dishes in her family's tent twenty feet away. She is,
besides too young, and to my eye as I stand there in my ill-fitting
postmaternity clothes, too slender, a sort of wild English rose of
a girl, pale and wispy, wearing tan leather laced up the back into
some semblance of a corset, with a muslin skirt. It's all very "white
frontier woman caught by Indians," apparently caught just outside
Hollywood. We are not exactly getting a history lesson here.

Nor did we intend to. We came to the Cache Valley Mountain Man Rendezvous for the snacks — the beef jerky smoked
in someone's garage, the root beer brewed in someone's basement and slapped with labels that identify it as "Bison Brew,
Ogden, Utah." We know that Ogden is not a Rocky Mountain
trading outpost, but a blue-collar town with gang problems on
the populated corridor to Salt Lake City.

But historical rendezvous were similar to the present ones in their happy mayhem with an undercurrent of cynical beady-eyed materialism. Of course the mountain men were fur trappers and traders and as such were buying their yearly supply of guns and gunpowder, and sugar and coffee to last a year, not "vintage-style" calico baby bonnets, faux-horn-handled knives with dull edges, and snacks called Navajo tacos. I buy all these things, but I do it because this is really the only way I can take part. The people I truly envy at the rendezvous are the ones who aren't selling me anything.

Disallowed of buying, cheaply, for a day, into their way of life, I can only peer at them sitting around their campfires talking to each other heartily, familiarly. Never mind that the historical rendezvous happened for only sixteen years, meaning of course that many of these modern mountain men and women will have the opportunity to rendezvous more often than the nineteenth-century trappers themselves. This is now a membership ritual, a hobby that disallows casual participation: those who do not have period-authentic camping gear — canvas tents, iron cooking pots on the fire, blanket coats, leather trousers — must sleep away entirely from the main camp, banished to the parking lot. Those of us in jeans, wallets in purses, cameras slung over our shoulders, are more like ghosts, walking the dirt paths around the fires, peering wistfully in. All of my desire for membership, the fact that my daily front-window view is the backside of these very mountains, my spanking-new education in historical mountain men and rendezvous, put me no nearer participation than the most clueless of rubes here. Only commitment buys that.

We linger at the camp till late in the day, a hot early twilight as the sun tips over the high far edge of the rocks above. Rather than getting quieter as the visitors/shoppers leave, the camp awakens with roaring laughter around ever larger and more dangerous campfires, the ring of iron triangles calling people to dinner, musical instruments unrolled from blankets, shouts from one fire to another, the passing of gleaming brown glass bottles. The canyon echoes with the racket.

# LOTS FOUR AND FIVE, RANGE ONE WEST
## OF THE SALT LAKE MERIDIAN

................

I stand in the middle of what geographers call a desert surrounded by the tended pattern of tilled and irrigated land, snow-capped mountains, fat cows, clucking chickens. I picture the Hollywood intersection outside that front yard fence in Los Angeles, and I think, "Desert."

I sit on the back of my horse while he eats, next to the young son of our neighbor, who sits on the back of his horse while she eats, and who gave me the idea. We are equal parts supremely relaxed from our contact with the big wide backs of such contented chewing horses and giddy with having stolen an opportunity to be on them in the dead of winter. We are as silent as if our own mouths were full.

I see that through the snow I still recognize the highest field on the mountain by its hay bales, never gathered and now covered on their high side by snow. I recognize the difficulty of getting there — I've been there only by snowmobile, it's incredibly high — to till it, harvest it, gather it. I don't judge the waste. That man has made it so far up the mountain with his machines, well, I don't know yet if it surprises me or not.

More birth — and more death as well — happen to us here than I'd ever been privy to before in my life. I got pregnant, my cat got pregnant, my chickens laid fertilized eggs in spite of my best efforts, my goat arrived pregnant and had her unlikely kid here with us. So I guess I was taken aback, as if I knew anything, to discover that only elderly ladies have lived in my house half of its life. No babies were born in my house at all, nor raised here. I feel a strange sense of loss in discovering this, with a chunk of the history I'd invested in this place gone, a story I could connect to, the story I was living myself in the present. I regretfully, gingerly, loosen my emotional hold on my story of Johanna and her children here.

Planning and Zoning in City Hall is accustomed to requests like mine, these searches for pasts. I enter the town hall on Main Street, a revamped version of the classic four-square turn-of-the-century courthouse. Like so many of these western public buildings, the landscaping outside includes cannons; this one also features handcarts that replicate the ones pulled across the country by the original Latter-day Saints settlers. I haven't yet taken advantage of this, but I've noticed there are overnight camping trips that are reenactments of that arrival. In the promotional photos advertising the trip, entire families wear costumes and indeed pull a handcart over the granite rocks and creek beds of the nearby canyons and back country. The kids learn how very little actually can be brought in one of these carts — no televisions, for instance — and the parents learn a lot more than they bargain for, I expect; how shallow our own civilizing is, and the iron grip you have to keep on the instinct to wheedle and blame and shove, and how tender our feet will always be.

Main Street, as I enter the town hall, strikes me anew as Mayberry. Flowering trees line the green square. False Western fronts tower cheerfully over the still vibrant downtown storefronts. People honk only to wave hello. The teenagers who think they are being bad lounging on the public lawn share between them one cigarette.

This impression is in spite of the fact — is layered dissonantly over the fact — that I now know about the occasional meth problem in town, the sleeping around, the boys who have to get out and never come back to be who they want to be, whether they are gay or simply, as some of my students, want to be music majors instead of business majors preparing to support a family. That's all true; and yet I still have never been anywhere else with so little crime, so little litter, and so many people with the habit of being available when needed. The truth is that the industrious model of the Mormons seems to keep everyone on their toes, one way or another, toward or away from similar goals.

The ladies inside don't even ask for identification, for proof of my connection to this story, the day I come to untangle my house's past. When I see the way the records are kept I realize I am seeing how I myself appear and will always appear on the records of the home, in the tale it tells of itself on paper. It's all public record though the information seems intimate to me. Nearly before I've finished my question, a lady has turned a computer monitor screen my way, swiveling it over her stack of papers. "Is this you?" she asks. My name teeters at the top of a long list. Brief, brief years show my own timeline there.

Within minutes, I stand at a table alone with every scrap of the physical records of the house and land reaching back just over a hundred years. Bemused and appreciative of my appreciation, the ladies of the records office supply me with everything they've got on the block of land where my house stands. Graphed computer printouts back to 1986, typed lists fifty years back from there, and then an arm-length ledger, its paperboard covers curled by time and temperature, pages lined with fading green printed columns and the spidery ink-well dip sputter and scrawl of a few generations of record-keepers, all the way back to 1856 when Wellsville itself began, a slow-blossoming rash of houses and fences on virgin land.

Our lots, the west half of four and five, Block One of Plat B, Section Two, Township Ten North, Range One West of the Salt Lake Meridian, changed hands four times, presumably as farmland, probably for hay, until John S. Baugh bought it in 1897 (ownership beginning with the mayor, and I see here manifest destiny, come down to actual names, individuals, presumptuous, firm in their entitlement). I know from *Windows of Wellsville* that purchaser John Baugh had earlier married Elvira Bankhead Baugh in 1883, and they had one daughter, nine months and two weeks after marriage — and more than twenty years before the house was built. In 1897, two years after the purchase of this property, John was called on his second mission to England and by all accounts Elvira "worked hard to support her husband on the missions and support her daughter," selling "milk to Lorenzo Hansen's dairy."

Since no records were made of the actual building of houses, only of the transfer of land, I'm left to wonder, when precisely was the house built? My purchasing agreement says 1906. Did Elvira live in my house alone during those years of her husband's second mission, her daughter surely married by age twenty-three in those days and in Mormon country? Did John build Elvira a house and then leave her to it, hoping and dwelling on its protection, the state of it, during his mission abroad? Did Elvira milk those cows in our back pasture, in some early version of our milk house?

The land, with, presumably, a house on it, was sold in 1912 to Johanna Bailey, who had by then long since born and then grieved or raised each of her nine children. Widowed in the winter of 1910, what house was she leaving, to come to our small, apparently single-woman, solitary home? Was this a house of loss to her, of biding time, a shallow replacement for better, fonder memories? Or a cherished place of calm, to pass the last winters of her life in dignity? She lived here for no more than one year and eleven months, passed away gently at age seventy, and is buried in the Wellsville Cemetery next to the children she'd lost so young.

The few rooms of my mountain-lee house still murmur with memories, but in a different, sighing, introspective tone, not the ringing chime of voices I'd storied myself into believing. My family had brought both aspects as well, I guess, introspection and ringing voices, and so either was fine, as hauntings go.

Still, I am surprised at my disappointment. I have spent the year or two since being handed her photograph in imagining the children of Johanna running amok in my yard, sleeping soundly in my bedroom.

I do notice that as I read the heavy book on Wellsville from which I glean this information, rambling in its tone, lovingly compiled without the slightest nod to scholarly intention, paging through the biographies of people I don't know, whose names I've studied, whose relatives I sit next to at pot lucks and rodeos, that I read the folksy paragraphs as if they are stories: pausing at a photograph that looks especially modern, the couple in church-clothes black, faces and shoulders to the photographer but chins and eyes turned coyly in to each other, a smirk at the curve of the mouth, a stray unruly curl. I read their lives, learning their beginnings moments before I read their ends: divorce, I read, and wonder, with more urgency than perhaps I'm entitled as a nonrelative, why? Why, who did what, how to go from the private smirk of the photo to buried apart, when, why? What about the kids, where will you each be buried, why?

They had braided their lives, left a pattern for me to find, and then lived past the tidy version that indicates they lay happy and simply in the soil I'd invested with such meaning. But the stability I seek is in my own interest, my elaborate construction.

Most of what I read is in the end not surprising, not so unexpected; it's only that the moment I apply my *hopes* to the history, the record of people's lives will not behave.

# IN MY DEFENSE

.................

I am rambling, as I am wont to do, about citizenship, and mythology, and authenticity, employing a highly caffein-ated range of scholarly terms like "opacity of intention," and "cultural memoir," and "narrative research," and "rightly rejecting overt themes of entitlement versus belonging." In front of me, across a familiar table, sit three women I have grown to greatly admire. They are my master's thesis com-mittee. Between us is the knowledge of my having dragged myself in out of the haze of not-sleeping-through-the-night motherhood, and the luck of my having found a clean shirt to do this in. I am defending my thesis.

I like to think I am a friend of these three; being the oldest graduate student in their program by at least ten years helps, but we also share a common passion. Part of me wants to joke with them that if they don't pass my thesis, they'll have to bab-ysit my newborn while I rewrite it. But they don't make this process easy. My subject, the commercialization of the Western American myth, has to do in a roundabout way with them too.

One of them is currently fighting the city board about pro-posed development in the foothills near her home, which she argues persuasively should be levied with a conservation ease-ment. One of them is the editor of a foremost journal of West-ern literature scholarship, who long ago abducted her family from their East Coast roots to commit to this probably lesser-paying, more personally meaningful work in this region she loves enough for all of them. One of them was raised on a potato farm in nearby Idaho, on land her hopeful Czech grandfather filed for in the initial land-grant rush, which her family proceeded to lose the slow painful way for the next hundred years.

Me, I just moved in from Hollywood and started reading the books.

The conversation, bearing the weight of both my master's degree and my personal convictions right where these meet their own, is like trying to hold my breath while talking. They make me leave the room and let me sweat on the stairs for about twenty minutes. "How are you?" colleagues ask conversationally as they walk by me. "Pukey," I want to say. The women, my committee, tell me to come back in. "You really love this place," one of them says. "It made me sad, reading this, to see how much you don't want to go."

"Are you going to a PhD program?" they ask.

"What are you going to do?" they ask.

"Is there anything here for you to do?" they ask, three smart and tenacious women making less than their colleagues in more temperate climates, who know damn well their department has no PhD program in this, who got their advanced degrees and then made their way back here, who mouth off in their small department often enough to influence just enough of the outcomes so that they earn enough to stay, who well know the trade-offs of being here and being gone.

# VISION UPON VISION

.................

The clicking and whooshing sounds of magpies and pheasants outside my open window, beyond my waving curtain, almost but don't quite mask the murmuring of my infant daughter in the next room. The passing of time has gained momentum with its own weight: I can already tell I would relive each hard and precious day with my girl two or three times before moving on, all her life, if it were up to me.

It was much easier to imagine leaving this place a few months ago, hunched tightly against the cold with our backs to the mountain, when the lilac bushes looked like nothing more hopeful than fire starter, clumps of sticks instead of armloads of flowers.

I was hugely pregnant when the moving choice was made (stated passively, notice, as if it were not made by me), and not so much in a slow-blossoming-of-life way, but more of an all-my-body-and-mind-in-service-of-protecting-my-middle-bulk-against-the-slip-of-ice-and-searing-of-wind way. All turned in, and not outward. Much easier then to imagine leaving this place I love, as long as that or any action would result in lying down for a long, long nap.

A few summers, a few falls, springs, and lovely long winters, and I am leaving. Life seems to be making me go, but of course that is not true, the idea that I'm not complicit in the choice. I'm leaving for more graduate school, a PhD program in Ohio.

I know. This feels wrong. But there is life, and there is making a living. Sometimes these two do not dovetail gracefully together, no matter how hard we close our fists, grit our teeth, and pray. When they called to offer me a position from Ohio, I was holding a four-week-old baby on my lap. I was gazing out my kitchen window at my mountain with nothing short of joy. But I said yes.

Leaving is an experiment.

I can only say, and I am amazed to say it: I have never before left a place I loved. Always finished with the people and sights, the responsibilities and the mistakes, dissatisfied with the place or myself within it. Always urged by a better idea, and usually downright bored.

I'd had no idea what I was feeling now, even as I was living it, calling it fascination and mistaking it for research and not knowing it was love. I always said, before I moved here, that it would take something huge to make us stay, some sign that would indicate that terminal degrees were less important than this home. I'm afraid now that if that sign happened, I must have missed it, single-minded as I can be. Maybe I was looking too hard, thinking too big, not trusting the simple answer in my blood.

Maybe I didn't believe in the power of forward momentum. But here we are, preparing to leave. I'm afraid I've made a horrible mistake, and I can't believe I got Christopher to agree to it.

Of course, for him, being closer to family is most important. And the rolling hills and trees of the southern Midwest remind him of upstate New York, where he was raised. He never had the love I do for harsh land, land one has to work toward understanding; just the other day I sighed (dramatically, I'm afraid) across some gray-gold fields in Idaho: "I'll miss these long views." "Oh," he said, "there's beautiful views there." He meant without buildings; I meant without trees. To imagine my views circumscribed by rings of trees and short slopes of gentle hills, rising so easily to one's step, so spoon-fed a landscape, all curves and no lines, feels claustrophobic from here. I can only hope I am wrong, that some love waits in the creases of hills and undergrowth of trees that I don't know yet.

I'd already flown to southern Ohio, in the flats of Appalachia, to search for a house. The wall of humidity, the vines hanging off highway billboards, the click of frogs from ponds in every other field, felt like a foreign country to me. But this is America, I heard myself thinking. And I'm from around here, right? Still, I cried when my plane got back over the desert, when I could breathe again, over spines of rock again, knowing I was going to have to leave it all.

And so an assessor has recently been to our home in Utah, as a preparatory step to placing our house on the market. This seems infeasible while I'm living it: that a *home* can be sold, the dense weft and weave of this air, this solid clenching handful of life. But the assessor stopped his car in the middle of the road, walked past Christopher, and stood open-mouthed at the street's dead end, gazing rapt not at the house but at the mountain. "I've driven through Wellsville dozens of times," he said, "but I've never been on this street." This is a good sign, assessment-wise, as it means "private."

"Yes," I tell him. "We see as many horses go by as cars."

"This view," he tells us wonderingly, gravely, "is extremely rare," and he turns his head to take in the busy chickens, the placid cows, the scattered presence of cottonwood trees, the lack of neighbors. In assessment-speak, this means "worth a bunch of money."

My heartbeat suddenly feels like there's something wrong with it. Remind me: why am I leaving this? "Why are you selling this?" he in fact asks, bewildered. I step inside the house to stare in blank confusion at the walls and let my husband deal with the talking. Why are we selling this? What will someone else pay for our dream, the way we paid so hopefully a few years ago, and why are we selling it? Are we sure we can get that hope back when we call for it later, anywhere but here, any time but now?

We'll find out. We'll be back, we'll be back, we'll be back.

I hear the man say over and over, as if trying to convince himself, "Of course, this is an exceptional day." He means that the air is so clear, the sky so sunny, the mountain so perfectly snow-capped, that the view is postcard worthy, which must be a coincidence timed with his presence. No, I want to tell him, this isn't exceptional. The mountain looks that close, that sight-filling, that mysterious, that mouthwatering every day. It calls and answers.

That the view is worth money is insulting to me, that someone else may buy my kitchen window full of mountain and rip it down, realign a new monstrous dwelling to "maximize" that view, and cart away as junk the boards and plaster where I lived. My old house is a constant project, not the move-in most of the local new subdivisions are building, I know. But I am kept in mind of a book I'd read in class the last semester, which my classmates may have seen as homework but I'd begun to willfully read as parables, named *Staying Put*. Scott Sanders wrote that "mortar and nails alone would not have held the house together even for sixty years. It has . . . needed the work of many hands, the wishes of many hearts, vision upon vision, through a succession of families."

I would like my little family not to be the last on the record for this house. Being the last people to live inside this house would seem to represent a failure of stewardship on my part, and a dismantling of my own memory.

And I do want my memories. These are holding me to the earth.

# COWBOY UP

................

The horse is gone. We have stared at the paddock and into the barn long enough to make ourselves believe it, even though it seems impossible.

And when your horse is gone, it must have got out of the fence, they do that, so we wander the roads next to the house and down to the reservoir. We shield our eyes and peer down into the holler, and across the fields of cows. The horse is more gone than usual.

Shorty the pinto horse stands silently looking at us. She is not whinnying now, so having the palomino horse gone is not new news; Shorty is over it. How long has the other, Pal, been gone? All day?

Christopher calls Gail, Bill's wife. Bill gave Christopher this horse, in exchange for an undetermined amount of welding work on Bill's paddock fences, and it is hard asking Gail if she knows where the horse her family gave us has got to.

"He took it back," Gail says without hesitation.

"I'm sorry, what?" Christopher says into the phone. We are staring through our backyards toward their house, the way Bill must have done that morning waiting for us to leave.

"He gave you the horse for welding, which he doesn't feel you've done much of, and now you're leaving, so."

After Christopher hangs up, we stare at each other, unsure whether we feel embarrassed or angry.

"Well, how much welding did he expect me to do?" Christopher asks me. "I built a paddock. With six gates. I was there every evening for a month."

I don't have an answer, of course.

"More," I say, uselessly.

# FOUNDERS' DAY

. . . . . . . . . . . . . . . .

I t is the kind of perfect weather that you never can remember well later, only because it is exactly like your skin when you are happy; not too hot or cool, not wet or parched. It's the kind of weather that has kids playing in the background and the occasional parade. Late July mornings, in the shade of the town green, in the Rocky Mountains, run about sixty-five degrees.

We are in line for the pancake breakfast, but not because it will be good. We feel very pleased with ourselves that we knew what the cannons meant this year at dawn; that first year, when we told Bill later we'd heard cannon fire, he laughed because no one had remembered to tell us what it meant, no one had warned us it just meant pancake breakfast by the volunteer fire department.

No craning my neck to see what the holdup is. No twitchy foot stamp when a child drops his plate at our feet. I am slowing down: it is what it is. The gal from down the block, the one with three kids who is getting a divorce against her will, whose husband I saw necking down at the river with someone who was not her, waves a pie in the air at me before she sets it at the dessert table.

"Hi, folks," the ward bishop says heartily from behind us in line. His horses are shod in our barn. He will be relieved to not be bishop soon, to relax with his family. The two neighbor women, one who waved the pie and her next-door neighbor who is the one who goes running pushing her twin stroller and is the envy of all of us for the way she makes time out of thin air, join us all in line.

"What's your husband doing now?" the bishop asks the runner.

"Exotic dancer," she answers.

We all know he left his job at one of the car dealerships in town; he's trying to start his own. "Is he renting the lot out on the highway?" the bishop presses.

"Yep. We'll see."

Indeed, the food is not good, but we all pile our plates with it. Cold pancakes and slightly congealed sausage. Bread warmed and passed off as toast. The mountain climbs on our west side and the sweep of small road near our picnic tables comes in from the highway, past the Burger King, past the U-Haul rental, past the pasture that floods every spring, and the wooden sign at the edge of town that reads, "Wellsville, established 1856: the oldest permanent settlement in Cache Valley," under which lie lovingly tended tulips with a longer season than it seems like science can explain. Last spring the local volunteer firefighters rescued calves in an assembly line from the flooded field. They passed them hand to hand from the low land by the river up to the dry scrub end on a hill, yelling at the man who owned the cows after he showed up. They yelled as they passed calves to each other, the calves holding still in surprise, passing the owner in midair as he sat sputtering on his ATV. "You know this will happen," the volunteers yell. "This happens every year at snowmelt. It rained last night, it's already spring, get out of bed. That's the math."

After breakfast, we go find a spot near the horseshoe pits.

We spend most of the rest of the day there sitting on a blanket. Nobody from the university is down here in Wellsville. Of the neighbor's kids who spent so much time with us when we arrived, including here at Founders' Day the first year, the eldest got married, and divorced; the middle child, a girl, left to be a ski bum in Colorado; and the youngest boy got tattoos, and a motorcycle, which he came to show Christopher one chilly night at midnight when he saw the light on in the house. They talked about motorcycles, and through motorcycles, everything, for an hour, each taking turns sitting on the brand-new bike in the dirt road. The people who come to talk to us this year are a combination of the tattooed local kids who've grown up and had kids, and the Mormon families who didn't fall off the wagon and so didn't hang out with those other kids in high school.

Here they nod to each other, cautiously, over our blanket.

# MONUMENT TO BELIEF, MIDDLE OF NOWHERE, UTAH

................

I hold my daughter in the shade of my own body, the brunt of the midday sun on my back, and shift her away just slightly to let a breeze pass between her hot self and my shirt, under which I sweat in sheets. She rests her usually lively head on my shoulder and waits drearily for the train whistle to terrify her again. Still I don't regret this long drive, dragging my family to a visitor's center in the middle of this vast field of rocks, dirt, and memory, where green is like a mirage in the distance: walk up to the green and it dissipates into sparse cheat grass, brittle silvery sage, the small Russian thistle bushes that die to make tumbleweeds.

I am in a last-ditch race to gather memories, make the valley's public memories my own reserve. And it suits my present state of disbelief and sense of imminent loss, the unlikely nature of the enterprise here outside Corinne, Utah, the harsh land where this monument to belief stands. I stand now where the cross-country railroad was completed on men's backs from both coasts, finally, to here, which now we call Golden Spike National Monument, an act that was hailed nationally as the closing of the frontier forever.

What a flush of pride workers must have felt, with the eyes of America on them, this ragtag team drawn from "the vast pool of America's unemployed," a "volatile mixture" known for "drunken bloodshed," led by ex-army officers who had just been left jobless by the end of the Civil War. Was it a combination of media attention, cool weather, no liquor, the proximity of completion, that rushed the Central Pacific crew through laying ten miles of railroad track on April 28, 1869? In the stifling convection oven heat of summer and often early spring in the desert, a breeze takes on existential, poetic, uplifting life, the rise of the hair on your neck a murmur of hope, maybe enough to hurry you through backbreaking work, to keep you thinking of home, better places, women and bedsheets, river water, shade, laying down the shovel, the pick, the dynamite. Anyway, it seems to indicate a reprieve. And April of 1869 may have been full of such days. Or, well, it may have been downright cold. So goes the high country desert.

Before the loudspeakers begin the sudden yammer of orchestrating my experience, I imagine only the sound of the "grand anvil chorus" ringing here, the shouting and swearing of men, the sliding of metal across dust. As the announcer directs me and the small crowd I stand with to notice the escaping steam of the reproduction locomotive, as the reenactors climb up to start stoking the coal and wood bins that drive the machines, I'm amused to note that no amount of script reading and picture taking can override the present reality of the heat and space of the surroundings. It's the kind of place of which my husband, bless him, says on getting out of the car, "This is effing *nowhere*." Which it is adamantly not, by nature of this event if nothing else, but if it were, it is a big and un-ignorable, impressive nowhere. And so in being brought to focus on the small stretch of track in front of us, the reproduction of the very notch where so many historical photos prove what we had done, the photos of white rich financiers somberly shaking hands as if they'd just built a railroad, surrounded by wearily grinning bedraggled white workers, surrounded off-camera by crouching Chinese men and Indians — the huge backdrop stands in, in my mind, in larger ways than literal, for all we can't see in the photo. But it is amusing and poignant to look down at the spot and to stand on the place, at the reproduction stake made of real iron, in the same giddy way that the men themselves must have the day the ceremonial spike was driven in. Look what we built. Look what we did. We have spanned a continent; we have closed the frontier.

Perhaps due to the predictable nature of inevitability, the day that the golden spike was symbolically tapped is less interesting — and implicitly sadder — to me than that record-breaking April day the men lay ten miles of track. I know that the railroad meant the standardizing of time across America, an aggravating process that was something like herding cats. I know that the telegraph lines were strung by the railroad workers as they went, an upright mark on the land as important as the vertical stroke below it, and I picture the line and the track lacing in tandem through empty land as far as the eye can see, lovely and treacherous. Because of course the railroad means that more whites than the natives can repel and contain at a time will unload and disperse everywhere. The railroad means the seas of buffalo will have begun a rapid and ignominious decline to their end. The shortsightedness of our forefathers begins with alacrity to be very clear, gathering speed at the pace of a steam locomotive.

But the Central Pacific crew and the Union Pacific crew building their railroad didn't know, care, or think about any of this. The American public checked their newspapers daily for the progress of the tracks (reported back by those telegraph lines). The men had been laying the track for four years. The two companies, before the government was forced to intervene, had laid roughly two hundred and fifty *miles* of parallel track, passing each other toward the opposite coast, each company making money off the process, each man keeping a job.

In early April of 1869, Union Pacific laid eight and a half miles of track in a day. A simmering contest that till then had been unofficial became specific: Union Pacific bet the Central Pacific crew $10,000 (imagine what that would be with inflation adjustment) that they could not lay more than that as fast. They were wrong.

This contest is why I try to picture the weather that day. I want to know how long the CP workers stopped for lunch, if they woke up knowing today was the day of the attempt, if they clapped each other on the back, if they rallied each other out loud. They are so human like this. They are so alive. These are, after all, our great-grandfathers.

I take a boring picture of a sign that describes the parallel track building, and the competition — but only because I can't re-create the day of the contest and I can't be there the way I want to, and I can't tell by looking around where the double sets of tracks lay. I would like to look at that ground, see how close or far the lines were, and have a laugh as the workers might have every morning, nodding to the neighboring crew.

After the reenactors have climbed down and walked away, after the locomotives are still again from their show run around in a circle, the monsters cooling and rustling back into a drowse, the people visiting seem at a loss. They read the placards. They gaze at their digital camera screens to see if they've just miraculously managed to capture the scope of the scene still starkly and irrevocably spread before them. We all browse the gift shop, perhaps to buy proof we drove this far from "last highway service." We find a Western Meadowlark stuffed toy that sings its distinctive trill when pressed on the belly. We examine the maps, the old photos, museum cases of pocket watches of conductors, archival press releases, all the while eying the shimmer of the hugeness outside the large windows. Later, far from there, I will press the meadowlark's belly, because of course I had to have one, and wish I were back. It's very simple there, and plain in its loveliness, and just uninviting enough to probably never invite change — not again, like lightning striking twice on the same spot.

My husband won't even take the turn in the car to go to Promontory Point, the small town often conflated with the Golden Spike National Monument (but only if you're looking at a map instead of standing there). He indulges a lot of my impulses in the name of research — "I have to reread that sign, back up" and "Hold the baby/backpack/dog leash, I have to pick that plant" — but even he draws the line here, hot, tired, keeping his eye on the time bomb of a baby's needs and, frankly, probably bored of all the "nothingness" around us. The town lies over the bare land easily in sight down a surveyor's straight shot of a road, a dusty huddle of shelter, and I'm the only one in the car who wants to see that up close. Promontory Point was a town for a minute, in 1869, and then it was not, again. That's the story of a lot of places, it turns out. We race in our modern car, picking up speed back into the present, back to highway services, back to a cool lunch for baby, back to the air-conditioning, back to the future.

# 5

# CULLING SEASON

Loss is the great lesson. But happiness, when done right, is a kind of holiness, palpable and redemptive.

MARY OLIVER, "POPPIES"

# SHOOTING STARS LIT UP THE YARD

.................

I dream I'm lying in the garden where the dogs are buried, looking up through the box elder tree above us all. I have begun to dream slowly, with all five senses and in detail, every bit of it as minute as a cat's sandpaper tongue and as tactile as metal in winter. I can describe the porous concrete of the back stoop, and where it is breaking away from the back wall and where the rainwater pools. I can feel the paint chipping under my hand on the warm metal swing outside, where the last owner hung his dressed deer to drain out ("the saddest swing in the world," one of my clever and vegetarian friends from L.A. had quipped before we moved, the two contexts butting heads, and I still remember how teetering it felt to be on that edge, between the sentimentality and the practicality). I can see the wooden shingles under the back left corner where the siding had lost its cap, maybe encouraged by my prying. I can feel the black on blackness of the horses swimming near the fence in the middle of the night, benign sharks rising to the surface of dark water and then curving languidly away back into the depths; I know what the soft pine floors look like under the kitchen linoleum and where the builders cheated in its repair, can feel the cool and thick interior wall of the addition between the 110-year-old main room and the 100-year-old kitchen; can smell the iron kettle on the wood-burning stove in the fireplace surround; can show you where my baby laid her head every night of her life to date, and where the bones of two dogs lie near the vegetable garden I tended until I hated the sight of a weed, a hose, or a bean. I can hear the sound of the creek a mile away, fueled by snow run-off all year. Picture every night when the moon lit up the mountain, and shooting stars lit up the yard, and I pressed my face to the window screen, watched the horses steadily swim in their sea of black air, and the shadows of calves come loose from their own nearly theoretical fence to stand calmly on the dirt road. I can listen again to husband and baby stir in their beds, and smell the cold air, and remember I always could tell what the weather would be tomorrow by the timbre of the wind at night.

The major coffee chain did come to town, not a year after I wrote that it had not yet. The place still echoes hollowly most of the time, however, not yet having metastasized into the cultural zeitgeist of village squares it represents in Los Angeles. I am very proud of the valley for this. The major movie rental chain opened and closed down, apparently not due to lack of profits but to lack of interest on the part of the owner. Again, this makes me proud. Wellsville itself is surrounded, literally surrounded on all sides, not by fields now but by housing developments with names like "Heritage Fields" and "Wellsville Ranch," no doubt indicative of what they've each replaced. Naturally, this has not nor could it ever blot out my mountain view, from our valley floor at an altitude of 4,500 feet rearing its head 5,000 additional feet, the steepest vertical rise of mountain on the continent. It does temper the wildness, however: the practical cars and tidy roofs and illogical lawns sitting on the apron of this beast.

My third year of Founders' Day, I did get up to hear the cannons but either the man driving the flatbed truck missed our block or I, inexplicably, fell back asleep. Being pregnant could be an excuse but not, I think, a good one. After all, cannons! I did watch and adore the annual Sham Battle, but I was not near enough to the loudspeakers to hear what explanation was given this year for the beatdown of the Indians. Anyway, if anyone was watching closely, the Indians actually won, as they always do here at the grade school baseball field. I found out, by the way, that the loudspeakers and historical speech routine is only three years old, beginning exactly the year I first attended, not an age-old tradition as I'd imagined. I like to picture the battle, the disorganized and frenzied circling of the ball field, happening without explanation, without translation, just happening because this is what happens after the parade, a Rorschach test of occasions. The bright red womenfolk this year had ordered black heavy wigs to cover their straw blond hair. Christopher placed third in the festivity's horseshoeing competition, to the chagrin of the good old boys who practice all year in their backyards, telling stories slowly over their plastic cups of root beer and Sprite.

Bill, in the end, did not come to say good-bye to us. Somehow, slowly, we had betrayed the hope he must have had for us to change his mind about city people. I never did ride that horse he chose for me often enough, and that must to him have seemed a sinful waste of money and intention. Christopher didn't do enough neighborly welding on Bill's horse fence after he had started grad school; more play rehearsals, less neighboring. The rest of the neighborhood had liked us fine, but we took and failed Bill's own cowboy character test, and I don't know what that means about us. Other neighbors had started over time to tell us more about how "idiosyncratic" Bill was, but I never could quite determine if they meant his laconic, old-fashioned ways or some other less romantic, more clinical thing. Another year or so of paying attention and learning the locals might have told. It is exactly the sort of reason I wanted to stay still. I don't even know what test we took, so I can't tell if it matters to me that we failed it. In truth, though, we figure he mostly didn't want his old horse Pal to leave the valley, and we would have wanted the same for her ourselves.

The Relief Society Women's Organization of the Third Ward gave me a baby shower. While for them it was also part of their "service," hours they are required by duty to religion to fill doing for others, and is something they also do with professional precision and zeal, it meant a lot to me. Just noting how much we had to talk about with each other, compared to when I'd moved there and been invited anxiously to picnics, was amazing. For better or worse, the word was out that I would be moving, and they were lovely in spite of it, only giving the most veiled of threats, as in: "Is your property subdivide-able? I hope not, not in *Wellsville.*" This in spite of most of them living on plots that less than a hundred years ago were owned and farmed by a single man, who sold the adjoining land as he saw fit, piece by piece. It seems this house was the only one here within a quarter mile and faced with very little company the low rolling foothills then covered in fields of grass hay and alfalfa, where the ladies' houses would later stand. How ironic now that as a newcomer I'd been the only one willing to live in such an old house.

Apparently, though, I'm not alone in knowing I'm part of the problem, in changing the thing that I love for its mythic "unchangeability" — the ladies and I seem to share an unrealistic sense of "let me in, but close the gate behind me." But anyway, if we thought this region was unchanging, we were fooling ourselves. We are all proof that it is not, just as every wave of immigration has been: immigrants, missionaries, trappers, white men, schoolmarms, extended families, conservationists, outdoor enthusiasts, celebrities, California expats.

When I got home from the baby shower, half my chickens were dead, killed by a dog out for an evening run next to his owner's slow-driving truck. I cried hard, but privately, having raised those chickens by hand from downy chicks, yet still unsure whether one was allowed to feel so much for such a stupid and small animal that lives a half-acre from you in your barn anyway.

The day after that Mandilyn brought me a cake. Across its top was a whole diorama: Easter Peeps sugar chicks, strewn across tan dirt-colored icing, ominous tiny headstones tilting behind them. I laughed so hard I cried, and then I kept on crying for a bit more. We ate the cake gleefully, Christopher telling and retelling his own traumatic story of trying urgently to pick up all the feathers fluttering across the paddock before I got home, while the owner of the dog had yanked his dog up into the truck bed and then crawled through the fence and started to pick up chicken parts too.

But then just the other morning I walked out into the barn to the sound of cheeping. One chick stood alone, surrounded by faintly chirping eggs, other chicks about to be born. We've started the closing-down of things, the wrapping-up of one life to look forward to another, no matter how unwilling on my part, because finally the trucks are coming for our stuff and there's packing to be done. Those remaining chickens did not care about any of that. The mission of chickens is always, will only ever be, living in the moment. They were pleased as punch to continue to sit on eggs, because we'd utterly forgotten to collect eggs. And we hadn't been lazy for long; gestation for chicks is a scant three weeks. Somewhere there was still a rooster.

I held the perfect warm eggs to my ear, rapt at the contained, ordained, confident cheeps within the shells. I spent the whole afternoon running back and forth to the barn, lay on my belly in the straw to watch the chicks that emerged, and mourned the one egg that never opened.

I would have loved to watch the chicks grow, watching them moving in ever larger circles further into our yard, my girl moving in ever larger circles closer to them.

I gave the chicks away, along with the hen that had sat the eggs, to a man that answered an ad, with my blessing. (Mandilyn had said not to worry, I'd get dozens of calls for them, and I did.) Our nearest neighbor, the one who'd introduced herself the morning we moved in and offered to make us pancakes, has recently threatened the lives of our remaining brood. "Sorry to hear about your chickens getting killed during your baby shower," she said. "You know they're ruining my garden beds." And a day later, "Just wanted to let you know, I've put Round-Up and herbicides on the garden. You won't want your other chickens on that. FYI." With a smile as sweet as the morning we'd met her.

This says something to me about Wellsville. It says maybe it's okay to leave now. The yards that once held cows on Main Street, and the small fields between homes, will surely fill with houses, or at the very least the present houses will fill with people who say they are buying one way of life but are used to another, and they will vote and be vocal accordingly.

That being said, we won't be moving the remaining chickens with us, no. Even I draw the line somewhere before that; they'll go to Mandilyn and James's farm. We've long since sold the goats, as they were ear-splitting demanders of good alfalfa hay, not the weed-eaters we'd been promised (granted, that habit was our fault, not the goats'). I'll probably sell Shorty the horse because her hoofs grow into the flat shape of dinner plates and she has what they call parrot mouth, both issues just bothersome enough to warrant not buying a trailer for her, to move her halfway across the country. I simply haven't fallen in love with her that much yet, and now I avoid her eye. The cat that came with the property, the ladylike three-legged cat that was feral when we arrived, will be coming to Ohio, and will not greet another stranger hopefully from her makeshift back door. We have grown surprisingly attached.

The dogs are coming, that goes without saying. That's family. One dog is new since we arrived, a border collie–retriever mix whose inexhaustible spirit and grin, in my mind, represent the optimism and outdoorsy workaholic git 'er done attitude of so much of the West. One lone dachshund, Dolly, will make her sixth move with me. Honey and Gus remain behind, consigned in peace to the dirt of our house yard. The living dogs were unaffected by the deaths; nature takes her course. On the other hand, for me, leaving my most familiar companion and Christopher's shadow behind here is very hard. More than the birth of my daughter, who was conceived here but who after all we are bringing with us, these dogs will always represent the serious slice of heart I leave behind. They'll be still next to this good old house where so much living happened, under my mountain view, out of the wind. The possibility of what may someday happen to their remains seems to me a microcosm of what will happen to the valley; it is another reality I try not to dwell on, one that pains me more than is sensible.

But my daughter will know that any animals she takes on — which she should do, and reach far outside the natural myopic selfishness of residing in one's own skin — are her lessons in life and in death. Animals will be dependent on her, and that is a very fine obligation to have, and this is a lesson about humans as well. We've been left alone, ultimately, with many life-or-death moments, which I feared so much when we had the birthing of Dude the goat on our hands. Many small animals were raised here with great care. A dozen chickens, two kittens, and two magnificent dogs all died on our watch here. One sweet baby was born.

Still, we have not spent much time in this place that will change me forever. My briefest recap is only that I kicked a few rocks around, met a few people, slept under the bright stars, buried some dogs, lived with a new husband, birthed a baby, and the West simply swallowed all that whole. That is what nature and time do. That's the math.

We cannot change how inalterably simple we are, us humans, and animals too, and for that matter grasses and trees: finite in scope and time, like days.

But what a vessel we are.

With all my high hopes for a new life, a sort of witness protection program of ex-urbanites who knew too much and yet knew so damn little, I never could have convinced anyone from within a thousand miles of here that I was anything but what I am, beginning as a fish out of water and ending with an uneasy but abiding love — even in riding boots, even knowing the names of every family buried in the cemetery, even knowing what a holler and a draw and a crick are, I have been since I arrived the girl from California.

And I'm not even from California.

I'd guess I'll be forgotten by everyone in Wellsville. My face will disappear from their memories, and then our names, my husband and daughter and I, and then the evidence of the work of our hands on the property. I'm okay with that. I want to remember them, but they don't need to remember me for that to happen. Mostly I regret leaving the land, in the end.

I take a lot of walks that last summer, unwilling to go inside four walls that could be anywhere and will be Ohio soon enough. I walk Wellsville's little roads relentlessly, and the canyons, and circle through the pine trees and thistles of the town reservoir like a dog. I walk a lot in the last fields by the mountain, up above the riding arena, with the baby sleeping slung across my front and the dogs running down their familiar treads, out of my eyesight ahead in the tall grass. I think about the different dogs that ran this path with me when I first found it, exhilarated for all of us at the open space and finally learning to leave the leashes in the truck and the truck unlocked.

I tuck sage in my pockets, willing the scent to stay.

I eye the rock quarry spreading over the hill, eating permanently all the delicate land in its path. I turn north to see the housing development sneak near. I pray there are enough places where fields or meadows spread unchecked to mountains, as others pray that somewhere nature is allowed to run undeveloped to ocean. I must be able to see this field when I close my eyes, when I dream, because surely when I see it again it will not look like this.

And it doesn't.

# ACKNOWLEDGMENTS

················

I am grateful to the Charles Redd Center for Western Studies for a research grant on the dude ranch portion of this work. I thank Ohio University for its outstanding fellowship (and Catherine Taylor, who on a key year said "this one"), which allowed me time to write, earn a PhD, and raise a daughter concurrently. Thanks to Dinty W. Moore for his ongoing support and for helping me as I navigated a new experience even with my own enthusiastic foot so often in my mouth. I thank Utah State University faculty for blowing my mind at a crucial time in my life, namely Evelyn Funda and Melody Graulich, the influence of both of whom I can hardly find the words to credit.

Thanks to Ladette Randolph for asking to "see the book" when this was only a ten-page essay, the very first time I read a portion of it in public, promptly changing the direction of my life. Thanks to Kristen Elias Rowley for carrying the torch.

Thanks to the readers of my manuscript, the anonymous ones as well as Judith Kitchen and Mary Clearman Blew. Every bit of what I was told was helpful.

I'd like to also acknowledge the Western Literature Association for being my professional touchstone, both in terms of scholarship and conduct. By conduct I mean fond and engaged intellectual respect for others, an ingrained tendency toward interdisciplinary thinking, and a sustained commitment to a community.

Thanks to my parents, Wyatt and Dixie Stephens, and my in-laws, Tom and Fritch Martin, for their belief in this project, their patience with me in all ways, and their support, financial and emotional.

Thanks to Christopher for the endless ways he makes my life easier, and some of the ways he makes it more difficult, and for making that a good life. Thanks to Birdie, for making me aim to be a better person, when I might otherwise have given up and taken a nap on the couch, with a book across my chest, forever.

Finally, to the animals. Thanks for teaching me everything else. I am an ongoing student.

*Thoughts from a Queen-Sized Bed*
by Mimi Schwartz

*My Ruby Slippers: Finding Place
on the Road Back to Kansas*
by Tracy Seeley

*The Fortune Teller's Kiss*
by Brenda Serotte

*Gang of One: Memoirs of a
Red Guard*
by Fan Shen

*Just Breathe Normally*
by Peggy Shumaker

*Scraping By in the Big Eighties*
by Natalia Rachel Singer

*In the Shadow of Memory*
by Floyd Skloot

*Secret Frequencies: A New York
Education*
by John Skoyles

*The Days Are Gods*
by Liz Stephens

*Phantom Limb*
by Janet Sternburg

*Yellowstone Autumn: A Season of
Discovery in a Wondrous Land*
by W. D. Wetherell

To order or obtain more information
on these or other University of
Nebraska Press titles, visit www.
nebraskapress.unl.edu.